Haunted Airports:

Ghostly Tales, Unexplained Phenomena, and Eerie Encounters from the World's Most Mysterious Airports

By Lee Brickley

Copyright @ Lee Brickley 2023

Contents:

Introduction..5
The Phantom Pilots of Denver International Airport.......................9
The Crying Child of Heathrow Airport..17
The Lady in White at Madrid-Barajas Airport................................23
The Ghostly Aviator of O'Hare International Airport....................29
The Unsettling Apparitions of Kuala Lumpur International.........35
The Tragic Spirits of Tenerife North Airport..................................41
The Phantom Flight Attendants of Dallas/Fort Worth Airport...49
The Haunted Hangar of Los Angeles International Airport..........57
The Lost Souls of Charles de Gaulle Airport..................................63
The Ghostly Soldiers of Okinawa's Naha Airport..........................67
The Eerie Presence at Sydney's Kingsford Smith Airport...............73
The Haunting of Atlanta's Hartsfield-Jackson International........79
The Wandering Spirits of Newark Liberty International...............85
 The Haunted Halls of Berlin-Tegel Airport...................................91
The Phantom Flight of Amsterdam's Schiphol Airport..................97
The Unexplained Happenings at Toronto Pearson........................103
The Shadowy Figures of Rome's Fiumicino Airport......................109

The Eerie Whispers of Hong Kong International Airport............115

The Haunted Control Tower of San Francisco International....123

The Restless Spirits of Mexico City International Airport...........129

The Ghostly Encounters at Singapore Changi Airport...................135

Afterword...141

Introduction

Airports are bustling hubs of human activity, where millions of people pass through every day, each carrying their unique stories, dreams, and emotions. As we navigate these vast terminals, racing against time to catch our flights, or eagerly waiting for loved ones to arrive, we often overlook the hidden layers of history and mystery that lie beneath the surface. Airports are not just gateways to new adventures and opportunities, but also portals to the unknown, where the supernatural and unexplained intersect with our daily lives, creating an atmosphere that transcends the ordinary.

"Haunted Airports" invites you on a spine-chilling journey into the eerie world of ghostly encounters, paranormal activity, and supernatural phenomena taking place within some of the world's most renowned airports. From phantom pilots wandering the runways of Denver International Airport to the mysterious woman in white haunting the halls of Madrid-Barajas Airport, this book delves deep into the shadowy corners of these modern transportation hubs, unearthing the secrets that lurk just beyond the reach of our rational minds and challenging our understanding of the world around us.

Each chapter of this compelling book uncovers the chilling tales of a different haunted airport, meticulously exploring its history, architecture, and the events that have shaped its ghostly legends. Through extensive research, captivating firsthand accounts, and an unwavering commitment to unveiling the truth, we piece together the stories of the restless spirits that inhabit these spaces, forever trapped between this world and the next, and longing for resolution.

As you immerse yourself in the chilling narratives and eerie encounters contained within these pages, you'll gain a new appreciation for the power of belief and the persistence of memory. The tales within "Haunted Airports" serve as a testament to the idea that even in the most bustling, modern environments, the past can never be entirely left behind, and the echoes of bygone eras continue to resonate in unexpected ways.

While sceptics may dismiss these stories as mere urban legends or the products of overactive imaginations, the sheer number of accounts from credible witnesses is hard to ignore. From seasoned pilots and air traffic controllers to weary travellers and airport staff, the people who have experienced these hauntings come from all walks of life, united by their encounters with the inexplicable. Their testimonies, combined with historical records and expert analysis, paint a vivid picture of a world where the borders between the living and the dead are not as distinct as we might think, and where the supernatural lingers at the edges of our perception.

"Haunted Airports" is not just a collection of ghost stories, but an invitation to explore the uncharted territories of our own beliefs and perceptions. It challenges us to confront our fears and uncertainties, reminding us that sometimes, the most haunting tales are not those of restless spirits, but of the living who bear witness to them, forever changed by their experiences.

As you embark on this thrilling journey into the realm of the supernatural, prepare to question everything you thought you knew about the familiar spaces you've traversed countless times before. With every page turned and every haunting tale unravelled, you'll find yourself delving deeper into the unknown, exploring the mysterious, and seeking answers to questions that may never be fully resolved. One thing is certain: after reading "Haunted Airports," you'll never look at airports the same way again.

The Phantom Pilots of Denver International Airport

Denver International Airport (DIA), located in the heart of the Rocky Mountains, is the largest and one of the busiest airports in the United States. Covering over 54 square miles, it is a sprawling testament to human ingenuity and ambition, a place where millions of passengers traverse its terminals, runways, and concourses each year. And yet, for all its modern marvels and architectural splendour, DIA has become known for something far more sinister: a seemingly unending series of ghostly encounters, paranormal activity, and inexplicable phenomena that have earned it the title of "America's Most Haunted Airport."

The Phantom Pilots, as they have come to be known, are perhaps the most infamous of the spectral residents that haunt the airport's terminals and runways. These ghostly aviators, clad in their vintage uniforms and seemingly trapped in an endless loop of their final flights, have been reported by countless witnesses, ranging from airport staff to pilots and passengers. Their spectral presence seems to be a chilling reminder of the darker moments in aviation history, and an eerie manifestation of the collective fears and anxieties that have long been associated with air travel.

The history of Denver International Airport is one shrouded in controversy, intrigue, and speculation. Construction began in 1989, with the ambitious goal of creating the most technologically advanced airport in the world. However, as the years went by, the project was beset by numerous delays, cost overruns, and allegations of corruption, which led to growing public scepticism and frustration. The airport finally opened in 1995, more than a year behind schedule and at a staggering cost of $4.8 billion—nearly twice the original budget.

It wasn't long after the airport's opening that rumours began to circulate about the secret tunnels and bunkers hidden beneath its vast expanse. Conspiracy theories abounded, with some claiming that these subterranean passages were built as part of a clandestine government project, while others believed they were intended to serve as a shelter for the global elite in the event of a catastrophic event. Although these claims have largely been debunked, they have nonetheless fueled the airport's eerie reputation, creating an atmosphere of uncertainty and unease that seems to permeate its every corner.

The first reported sighting of the Phantom Pilots occurred in the early months of the airport's operation, when a member of the ground crew claimed to have seen a group of ghostly figures in vintage pilot uniforms wandering the tarmac late one night. Startled by their sudden appearance and the overwhelming sense of dread that accompanied them, the crew member quickly alerted his colleagues, but by the time they arrived on the scene, the apparitions had vanished without a trace.

In the years since that first encounter, the Phantom Pilots have been sighted by numerous witnesses, their spectral presence manifesting in a variety of forms. Some have reported seeing them in the airport's terminals, silently watching the comings and goings of passengers with a solemn, almost mournful expression. Others have encountered them on the runways, seemingly in the midst of pre-flight preparations, only to vanish into thin air when approached.

One particularly chilling account comes from a commercial pilot who was taxiing his aircraft toward the runway for takeoff. As he navigated the aircraft along the taxiway, he suddenly noticed a figure standing at the edge of the runway, dressed in a vintage pilot uniform and gazing intently at his plane. Despite the radio traffic from air traffic control, the pilot instinctively slammed on the brakes, certain that a collision was imminent. To his astonishment, the figure simply dissolved into the darkness, leaving him and his crew baffled and shaken by the encounter.

The identity of these Phantom Pilots remains a source of speculation and debate among paranormal enthusiasts, aviation historians, and airport staff alike. Some believe they are the restless spirits of pilots who perished in tragic accidents, their souls tethered to the airport and the skies they once navigated. Others argue that they are manifestations of the collective fear and anxiety associated with air travel, their ghostly presence serving as a stark reminder of the inherent risks and dangers that have long plagued the aviation industry.

One compelling theory suggests that the Phantom Pilots may be connected to the ill-fated Stapleton Airport, which was Denver's primary airport prior to the construction of DIA. Stapleton, which was located just a few miles from the current site of DIA, was the scene of several tragic accidents during its years of operation, resulting in the loss of numerous lives. Could the spirits of these fallen pilots have been drawn to the new airport, forever tethered to the skies they once soared and the profession they loved?

While the true nature of the Phantom Pilots may never be known, their spectral presence at Denver International Airport remains a chilling reminder of the airport's haunted history and the mysteries that continue to surround it. Each new sighting of these ghostly aviators adds another layer to the ever-growing body of evidence, suggesting that there is more to this bustling transportation hub than meets the eye.

The Phantom Pilots are not the only eerie encounters reported at Denver International Airport. Over the years, there have been numerous accounts of ghostly passengers, disembodied voices, and other unexplained phenomena that seem to defy rational explanation. Many of these incidents have occurred in the airport's underground tunnels and passageways, where the line between the natural and supernatural seems to blur, and the echoes of the past resonate with an eerie intensity.

One particularly chilling tale involves a group of airport staff who were making their way through a dimly lit tunnel late one night when they suddenly heard the unmistakable sound of footsteps echoing through the darkness behind them. As they quickened their pace, the footsteps seemed to grow closer, until they could feel the presence of an unseen entity breathing down their necks. Terrified, the group broke into a run, finally emerging into the relative safety of the terminal above. To this day, none of them can explain the source of the mysterious footsteps, nor can they shake the lingering sense of dread that has haunted them ever since.

In another instance, an airport employee reported encountering a ghostly woman in a long, flowing dress as she made her way through a deserted baggage claim area late one night. The woman, who seemed to be searching for something or someone, paid no heed to the employee's presence, her translucent form moving silently through the darkness before vanishing into the shadows.

These and countless other eerie encounters at Denver International Airport serve as a stark reminder that, even in the midst of our modern, technologically advanced world, there are still mysteries that elude our understanding and forces that defy rational explanation. As the stories of the Phantom Pilots and their ghostly brethren continue to circulate, they challenge our perceptions of the world around us, inviting us to explore the unknown and question the very nature of reality itself.

In the end, the haunting tales of Denver International Airport are not just a testament to the power of belief and the persistence of memory, but also a reminder that the echoes of the past continue to reverberate in unexpected ways, shaping our collective experience of the present. Whether these ghostly encounters are the product of overactive imaginations or genuine supernatural phenomena, they stand as a chilling reminder that, in the world of the paranormal, nothing is ever quite as it seems. And as we navigate the bustling terminals, walkways, and runways of this vast transportation hub, we do so with a newfound sense of awe and curiosity, acutely aware of the hidden layers of history and mystery that lie just beneath the surface.

The Phantom Pilots, ghostly passengers, and eerie encounters that have become synonymous with Denver International Airport serve as a chilling reminder that, even in the most modern and bustling environments, the past can never be entirely left behind, and the supernatural may be lurking just beyond the reach of our rational minds.

As we traverse these haunted airports, we are confronted with the tantalising possibility that the boundaries between this world and the next are not as distinct as we might think, and that the supernatural may be far closer to us than we ever imagined. We are reminded of the power of belief, the persistence of memory, and the inexorable pull of the unknown, as we journey deeper into the shadowy corners of our own consciousness and the hidden realms that lie beyond.

So, as you embark on your next adventure, whether it be through the bustling terminals of Denver International Airport or any other seemingly ordinary transportation hub, remember the haunting tales of the Phantom Pilots and their spectral brethren, and consider the possibility that the world around us may be far more mysterious and complex than we ever dared to imagine.

The Crying Child of Heathrow Airport

The story of the crying child at London's Heathrow Airport dates back decades, a heart-wrenching tale of a young spirit forever lost in its vast corridors. This chapter delves into the history of the airport and the numerous eyewitness accounts of the child's spectral presence.

Heathrow Airport, situated in the London Borough of Hillingdon, is the United Kingdom's largest and busiest airport. It opened its doors in 1946 as a small civilian airport, but over the years, it has grown into a sprawling aviation hub, with five terminals and handling over 80 million passengers annually. As the airport expanded, it became not only a bustling centre of travel but also a hotbed for ghostly activity, with numerous accounts of spectral figures and unexplained occurrences. Among these tales of the supernatural, the story of the crying child of Heathrow Airport stands out for its emotional depth and the sheer number of credible witnesses who have experienced its haunting presence.

The first recorded sighting of the crying child dates back to the 1970s, during the construction of Terminal 3. Workers on-site would often hear the distant sound of a child crying, seemingly coming from the terminal's empty corridors. The cries were so lifelike that concerned workers would pause their tasks to search for the source of the sound, but they could never locate the distressed child.

As the years went by and Terminal 3 became fully operational, the crying child seemed to have taken up residence within the airport's walls. Passengers and airport staff alike began to report encounters with the young spectre, usually late at night or in the early hours of the morning when the terminal was at its quietest. The ghostly child, said to be around six years old, would appear in the shadows, weeping and clutching a small, tattered suitcase. Its heartrending cries would echo through the terminal, leaving many who heard it feeling a deep sense of sorrow and unease.

These encounters with the crying child were not limited to a specific location within Terminal 3. Instead, the apparition seemed to wander the airport, appearing in various departure lounges, baggage claim areas, and even on the tarmac itself.

Regardless of where the spirit manifested, however, its cries were always unmistakable – a haunting melody of despair that pierced the air and left a lasting impression on those who heard it.

The most chilling accounts of the crying child come from those who have had close encounters with the spirit. In one particularly eerie incident, a female passenger was waiting for a connecting flight in the early hours of the morning when she heard the unmistakable sound of a child crying. Searching for the source of the noise, she spotted a young boy standing alone near a set of doors that led out onto the tarmac.

Concerned for the child's safety, the woman approached the boy, only to find herself staring into the face of a ghostly apparition. The boy's eyes were hollow and full of sorrow, his face pale and translucent. As she reached out to comfort him, the spirit vanished before her eyes, leaving her shaken and disoriented.

Numerous attempts have been made to uncover the identity of the crying child and the tragic circumstances that led to its eternal wandering within Heathrow Airport's walls. While definitive answers remain elusive, the most widely accepted theory centres around a catastrophic plane crash that occurred in the early 1960s.

The crash, which claimed the lives of over 100 passengers, left a deep scar on the airport and the community at large. Among the victims were several young children, and it is believed that one of these children became trapped within the airport's liminal space, unable to move on to the afterlife. The child's eternal cries are said to be a manifestation of its longing for the comfort and safety it was cruelly denied in its final moments.

Over the years, various paranormal investigators and psychics have attempted to communicate with the crying child, hoping to offer solace and help the spirit find peace. Some investigators claim to have made contact with the spirit, learning that the boy's name is Thomas and that he was travelling with his family when the tragedy struck. Unable to find his parents in the chaos of the crash, Thomas became lost and disoriented, eventually becoming trapped within the airport's spiritual confines.

These paranormal encounters have led some to believe that Thomas's spirit can only find peace if reunited with his family, who also perished in the crash. This theory has prompted several well-intentioned individuals to search for the resting places of Thomas's family, hoping to guide the spirit to them and finally put an end to its ceaseless crying. However, to date, no conclusive connection has been made between the spirit and any of the crash victims, leaving the true identity of the crying child shrouded in mystery.

The story of the crying child of Heathrow Airport has become an enduring part of the airport's lore, passed down from generation to generation and captivating the imaginations of travellers and airport staff alike. While some remain sceptical about the existence of the ghostly child, dismissing it as an urban legend born from the tragic history of the airport, others cannot shake the haunting memories of their encounters with the spirit.

The crying child serves as a poignant reminder of the hidden layers of history and emotion that linger within the bustling terminals of the world's airports. For some, it is a testament to the power of human connection and the enduring bonds that can persist even beyond the grave. For others, it is a chilling reminder of the darker aspects of human existence – the pain and suffering that can accompany even the most seemingly innocuous spaces.

As the story of the crying child of Heathrow Airport continues to be told, the spirit remains a haunting presence within the terminal's walls, its plaintive cries echoing through the corridors and tugging at the heartstrings of those who hear it. Whether a genuine supernatural phenomenon or simply a captivating legend, the crying child serves as a powerful symbol of the enduring impact of tragedy and the inescapable nature of human sorrow.

With every haunting tale unravelled, our understanding of the unknown deepens, and the boundaries between the living and the dead blur further. The crying child of Heathrow Airport stands as a testament to the idea that even in the most bustling, modern environments, the past can never be entirely left behind, and the echoes of bygone eras continue to resonate in unexpected ways. As we navigate the world's airports, chasing our dreams and seeking new adventures, it is worth remembering that sometimes, the most haunting tales are not those of restless spirits, but of the living who bear witness to them, forever changed by their experiences.

The Lady in White at Madrid-Barajas Airport

Madrid-Barajas Airport, now known as Adolfo Suárez Madrid–Barajas Airport, is one of the busiest and largest airports in the world. Located in Spain's vibrant capital city, it bustles with activity round the clock, serving as the primary gateway linking Spain with the rest of the globe. Yet, amidst this pulsating hive of human activity, exists an enigmatic presence that has bewildered and fascinated airport staff and passengers alike — the spectral figure of a woman in white.

The first known sighting of the Lady in White dates back to the 1960s, a time when Madrid-Barajas was rapidly expanding its infrastructure to meet the needs of Spain's booming tourism industry. The woman, always attired in a flowing white dress and shrouded by an aura of melancholy, was first spotted in Terminal 1, lingering near the departure gates in the dead of night. In the decades that followed, sightings of the Lady in White became a recurring phenomenon, fueling endless speculation and mystery.

According to eyewitness accounts, the apparition appears to be a woman in her mid-thirties, of medium stature with long, wavy hair cascading down her shoulders. Her face, although ethereal and translucent, is described as being of extraordinary beauty, often tinged with an unspeakable sadness. As witnesses recall, she always appears to be waiting for someone, her eyes scanning the crowds with an anxious longing that transcends the boundaries of this world and the next.

One such encounter was reported by a late-night janitor, who in the early hours of a winter morning, saw the lady standing near Gate 16, staring out into the empty tarmac, her figure bathed in the moonlight streaming through the windows. When the janitor approached her, intending to inquire if she needed assistance, the woman vanished into thin air, leaving the janitor stunned and with a story that would echo through the halls of Madrid-Barajas for years to come.

Yet another account comes from a seasoned pilot who, after landing his plane in the wee hours of the morning, spotted a woman in white on the runway. Alarmed, he reported the sighting to the control tower, fearing for the woman's safety. However, when security arrived on the scene, they found no trace of the woman. The pilot, a rational man of science, was left grappling with the inexplicable, his world view forever altered by this single, chilling encounter.

Despite these spectral sightings, the identity of the Lady in White remains shrouded in mystery. Some believe she is the ghost of a woman who was supposed to embark on a journey from Madrid-Barajas but met an untimely death. Others speculate that she might be the spirit of a grief-stricken woman waiting for a loved one who never returned from a voyage. These theories, while intriguing, are based largely on conjecture, leaving the true identity of the Lady in White an unsolved enigma.

The haunting of Madrid-Barajas Airport goes beyond mere sightings. There are reports of inexplicable cold spots near Gate 16, and the faint, ephemeral scent of a vintage perfume lingering in the air. Electronic equipment malfunctions without reason and objects move without any visible force. These uncanny events have led some to speculate that the airport is built on a ley line, a supposed alignment of the earth's magnetic field that is believed to be a conduit for spiritual energy.

As much as the Lady in White is a spectral entity, she has become an integral part of the folklore of Madrid-Barajas Airport. She is a constant, chilling reminder of the airport's layered history, a spectral echo resonating through the bustling terminal. To some, she is a symbol of unresolved longing and a testament to the airport's complex past, while others see her as a beacon of the unknown, her presence a stirring reminder of the mysteries that exist within the fabric of our daily lives.

Even in the face of technological advancements and the relentless march of progress, the Lady in White persists, a spectral anomaly in an age of rational thought and scientific understanding. Her existence challenges our conception of reality, forcing us to confront the possibility that there might be more to our world than what meets the eye. Her presence casts a long, eerie shadow over the airport, a ghostly imprint that lingers long after the last flight has taken off and the terminal lights have dimmed.

Despite numerous investigations and countless hours of research, the mystery of the Lady in White remains unsolved. Is she a figment of collective imagination, a ghostly echo of the past, or a genuine supernatural phenomenon? The answer remains elusive, buried deep within the hallowed halls of

Madrid-Barajas Airport.

Yet, her presence has left an indelible mark on the airport and its patrons. Those who have witnessed her spectral figure are forever changed, their perceptions of reality irrevocably altered. They carry her story with them, a haunting memory that transcends time and space, a chilling reminder of the airport's ethereal inhabitant.

As the sun sets and darkness descends upon Madrid-Barajas, the airport transforms from a bustling hub of human activity into a realm of spectral silence. It is during these quiet hours, when the world is in slumber, that she appears, a melancholic figure bathed in white, forever waiting, forever watching. In these moments, the airport belongs to her, a spectral monarch in her moonlit kingdom.7

Haunted by her unending vigil, the Lady in White at Madrid-Barajas Airport stands as a testament to the unseen mysteries that dwell within our everyday spaces. Her haunting tale invites us to question the nature of our reality and to explore the shadows that dance at the edges of our perception. As the chapters of "Haunted Airports" unfold, we delve deeper into these spectral narratives, venturing into the unknown and seeking the truth that lies just beyond the veil of our understanding.

The story of the Lady in White is but one of the many tales that echo through the corridors of Madrid-Barajas Airport. Each story, each spectral sighting, adds a new layer to the airport's rich tapestry of history and mystery, transforming it from a mere transportation hub into a portal to the supernatural.

The Ghostly Aviator of O'Hare International Airport

The city of Chicago, famed for its architectural marvels and vibrant arts scene, is also home to one of the busiest airports in the world - O'Hare International Airport. Situated on the city's far northwest side, it stands as a testament to the triumph of human engineering, a bustling hub connecting millions of passengers to destinations worldwide. Yet, nestled within this modern edifice, shrouded in the ebb and flow of daily activity, there thrives a spectral presence. This is the haunting tale of the Ghostly Aviator of O'Hare International Airport.

Like most ghostly phenomena, the story of the Ghostly Aviator finds its roots in the airport's history. The land on which O'Hare International Airport now stands was once the site of Orchard Place, a small farming community. In the 1940s, the area was transformed into an aircraft assembly plant and later an airfield named Orchard Place/Douglas Field, producing military planes during World War II.

The airport was later renamed O'Hare International Airport in honour of Lieutenant Commander Edward Henry "Butch" O'Hare, a Chicago-born naval aviator and the United States Navy's first flying ace during World War II. The transition from a quiet rural landscape to a buzzing military manufacturing site and finally to one of the busiest airports in the world, lends a complex, layered history to the land, an echo of the past that persists in the present.

The first reported sighting of the Ghostly Aviator dates back to the late 1970s, when an airport maintenance worker reported seeing a man dressed in a vintage pilot's uniform near one of the hangers late at night. Startled, the worker approached the man, who seemed disoriented and distressed, but before he could reach him, the figure vanished into the misty darkness.

Since then, there have been numerous sightings of the Ghostly Aviator, often appearing in the late hours of the night or the early hours of dawn. He is always described as dressed in a World War II era pilot's uniform, complete with a leather bomber jacket and a peaked cap. The figure appears solid and real, not translucent or ethereal as one might expect a ghost to be.

The Ghostly Aviator is often seen wandering around the runways and the old hangers, appearing lost and confused. There are reports of him looking at planes taking off and landing with an expression of deep longing and sorrow. Some say he seems to be searching for something - or someone - he left behind. The spectral pilot never interacts with the living, seemingly locked in his own world, forever trapped between the past and the present.

The identity of the Ghostly Aviator remains a mystery, fueling much speculation and intrigue. Some suggest he could be the spirit of a fallen World War II pilot, his restless spirit drawn to the place where planes were once manufactured. Others speculate that he could be a pilot who perished in one of the several plane crashes that occurred at O'Hare over the years, his spirit unable to move on.

While sceptics dismiss these sightings as the products of overactive imaginations or optical illusions, the consistency of these reports over the years, often by credible witnesses, lends a certain credibility to the Ghostly Aviator's existence. The sightings are not limited to any specific area within the airport but span across various terminals and runways, often in areas where the public has no access.

Interestingly, the Ghostly Aviator isn't associated with malevolent hauntings or poltergeist activity. There are no reports of him causing harm or inducing fear. He seems to be a benign entity, lost in his own spectral existence, a silent witness to the ceaseless progression of time and the relentless march of progress. He seems to be locked in a solitary dance with the past, forever tethered to the land that once bore the echoes of war and now resonates with the hum of modern aviation. His silent figure serves as a haunting reminder of the human lives embedded within the pages of O'Hare's vibrant history, the dreams that took flight from its runways, and the tragedies it has borne witness to.

The Ghostly Aviator of O'Hare International Airport, in his spectral solitude, brings to the fore the poignant intersection of the past and the present, the living and the dead. He highlights the uncanny ability of certain spaces, like airports, to become repositories of collective memory and shared experiences, transcending their mundane functionalities to embody the complex tapestry of human existence.

The story of the Ghostly Aviator is not just a chilling tale of a haunted airport, it is a narrative steeped in history, nostalgia, and an inexplicable yearning for something that has been irrevocably lost. It forces us to consider the legacies we leave behind, the echoes of our actions that might linger long after we are gone. It underlines the enduring power of memory and the uncanny ways in which it can shape our perception of places.

The Ghostly Aviator, with his spectral wanderings and his silent vigil, lends an eerie yet fascinating dimension to O'Hare International Airport. His haunting figure stands as a spectral beacon of the airport's layered history, the human stories that it cradles within its sprawling expanse, and the enduring mysteries it fosters.

To the casual observer, O'Hare International Airport might appear to be just another bustling transportation hub. But to those who have encountered the Ghostly Aviator, the airport is much more than that. It is a space where the past and the present collide, where the living share their space with the echoes of the dead, where every flight that takes off carries with it a piece of the airport's spectral legacy.

As we delve deeper into the world of "Haunted Airports,"

exploring the uncanny narratives and eerie encounters that populate these spaces, we are drawn into a realm that exists just beyond the reach of our rational minds. The haunting tale of the Ghostly Aviator invites us to question the nature of our reality, to challenge our understanding of the world, and to acknowledge the presence of the inexplicable within our everyday spaces.

Whether you believe in the existence of the Ghostly Aviator or dismiss it as an urban legend, the story serves as a poignant reminder of the intriguing mysteries that the world continues to harbour, often in the most unexpected of places.

The Unsettling Apparitions of Kuala Lumpur International Airport

Kuala Lumpur International Airport (KLIA), known for its sprawling terminals and striking architecture, a hub of human activity where millions traverse its polished floors each day, is also a place where the inexplicable and the supernatural seem to intersect with our waking reality.

The airport's history is a testament to the rapid growth and development of Malaysia as a nation. Opened in 1998, KLIA was a marvel of modern architecture and design. It was built on a site that was once an expansive palm plantation, a testament to Malaysia's agricultural past. As the palm trees were felled and the land cleared, the airport rose, a symbol of Malaysia's entry into the global stage. But as the airport grew, so did the tales of eerie encounters and spectral sightings, suggesting that the airport's impressive structures might not be the only things occupying the land.

Numerous reports have been made of shadowy figures darting across the expansive corridors of the airport, disappearing just as quickly as they appeared. Some have described them as fleeting, indistinct shapes, while others have spoken of more detailed apparitions, including a spectral figure of a man clad in a traditional Malay attire, his face obscured by shadows. These sightings have not been limited to the dead of night; many have occurred in broad daylight, with the figures seemingly indifferent to the bustling activity around them.

One of the most chilling reports came from an air traffic controller who reported seeing a shadowy figure on the runway in the early hours of the morning. According to his account, he was in the control tower when he noticed a figure standing motionless near one of the runways. He immediately alerted ground crew, fearing a security breach. However, when the security personnel arrived at the scene, there was no one there. The figure had vanished, leaving no trace of its presence.

Ghostly whispers and disembodied voices have also been

reported throughout the airport. These phantom voices often murmur inaudible phrases, but some have reported hearing their names being called, the voices echoing through the vast terminals. The source of these voices has never been identified, their origin as elusive as the spectral figures that haunt the airport.

Perhaps the most unsettling account comes from a group of late-night travellers waiting for a delayed flight. According to their reports, they were sitting in one of the departure halls when they noticed a group of figures standing near one of the gates. The figures were dressed in old-fashioned clothes and seemed out of place. As they watched, the figures slowly faded away, leaving the travellers in stunned silence.

These accounts, while intriguing, are also deeply unsettling, suggesting that KLIA, for all its modernity and grandeur, is also a place where the past lingers, where the veil between the living and the dead seems to thin, and where the supernatural is just as much a part of the airport as the planes that take off from its runways.

Such tales of hauntings and spectral encounters are not uncommon in places of transition, such as airports. It's as if the energy of countless goodbyes, reunions, arrivals, and departures somehow imbue these places with an otherworldly quality, making them fertile ground for encounters with the unexplained. And KLIA, with its mix of old and new, its roots in a past that has been paved over by the trappings of modernity, seems to encapsulate this paradox perfectly.

The apparitions of KLIA serve as a reminder of the history that lies beneath the airport's polished exterior, of the stories that were unfolding long before the airport was even a concept. They are a testament to the idea that some spaces, no matter how modern or mundane, carry with them echoes of the past, echoes that sometimes take on forms that defy rational explanation.

The eerie encounters and spectral sightings that have been reported at KLIA have transformed it into a place of intrigue, where the spectral and the everyday coexist. They speak to our fascination with the unknown, to our curiosity about what lies beyond the veil of our understanding, and to our capacity for wonder in the face of the inexplicable.

One late evening in January 2020, a traveller named Farah was transiting through KLIA. She had just arrived from London and was awaiting her connecting flight to Penang. As she strolled through the empty terminal in the wee hours of the morning, she noticed something unusual.

In a distant corridor, she spotted a group of women in traditional Malay attire, their faces obscured by shadows. They stood in silence, their figures reflected on the polished marble floor. Curiosity piqued, Farah decided to approach them, thinking they were part of a cultural performance. But as she moved closer, she felt a chill creep up her spine. The air around her turned cold, and she could hear a faint whispering sound.

Undeterred, Farah continued her approach, but as she neared the group, she realised something was amiss. The women were transparent, their forms shimmering like a mirage. Just as the realisation struck her, the figures turned towards her simultaneously. Their faces, previously hidden in the shadows, remained unseen, replaced by a deep, unsettling darkness.

Startled, Farah recoiled and blinked, rubbing her eyes in disbelief. When she looked again, the figures had vanished, leaving the corridor as empty and silent as before. Shaken, Farah hurried to the nearest occupied area, the whispering voices echoing in her ears.

Farah's story adds to the eerie tapestry of tales that surround KLIA. It embodies the unsettling blend of the ordinary and the spectral, the everyday and the uncanny that seems to pervade the airport. Her account, like the many others that have been reported, invites us to question our understanding of the world and to consider the possibility that there might be more to our reality than what meets the eye.

The hauntings of KLIA serve as a reminder that, in our fast-paced, hyper-connected world, there are still mysteries that elude our comprehension, phenomena that defy our logic, and experiences that challenge our perceptions. They invite us to look beyond the surface, to delve deeper into the realm of the unknown, and to consider the mysteries that lie just beyond the reach of our understanding.

The Tragic Spirits of Tenerife North Airport

Tenerife North Airport, also known as Los Rodeos Airport, is nestled among the verdant hills of the island of Tenerife, one of Spain's Canary Islands. Despite its tranquil setting, the airport is a haunting reminder of a tragic event that has left an indelible mark on aviation history. It was here, on the afternoon of March 27, 1977, that the deadliest accident in aviation history unfolded, claiming the lives of 583 people.

Two Boeing 747s, one belonging to KLM and the other to Pan Am, collided on the runway in a catastrophic accident attributed to a series of unfortunate circumstances including poor visibility due to fog, miscommunication between the pilots and air traffic control, and a regrettable decision by the KLM pilot to commence takeoff without explicit clearance.

The impact was devastating. The KLM plane exploded on impact, instantly killing everyone on board. The Pan Am plane, while not directly hit, was engulfed in a raging fire that claimed the lives of most of its passengers and crew. The few survivors of the Pan Am flight were those who managed to escape through holes in the fuselage before the fire consumed the aircraft.

The accident left a profound impact not only on the world of aviation, leading to significant changes in international aviation regulations and communication protocols, but also on the collective psyche of those who worked at and frequented the Tenerife North Airport. It was as if the weight of the tragedy had imbued the very fabric of the airport with an unshakable sense of sorrow and loss.

In the years following the accident, airport staff, passengers, and local residents began to report unusual experiences that suggested the tragedy had given rise to supernatural phenomena. The tales ranged from fleeting sensations of being watched or touched to more tangible manifestations such as unexplained sounds and apparitions.

One of the most frequently reported phenomena is the sound of muffled voices and cries, often described as resembling those of a crowd in distress. These unsettling sounds are said to be heard primarily late at night or in the early hours of the morning, and have been reported in various parts of the airport, including the runways, the terminal building, and even the parking lot.

Another common experience reported by witnesses is the feeling of an unseen presence. Many who have spent time at the airport, particularly after dark, have reported feeling as though they are being watched or followed, even when they are alone. Some have also described feeling a sudden, inexplicable sense of unease or dread, often accompanied by a drop in temperature or the sensation of a cold breeze.

Perhaps the most chilling of all are the sightings of apparitions. Over the years, numerous people have reported seeing spectral figures in and around the airport. The descriptions vary, but the figures are often said to be translucent and appear lost or confused. They are typically seen for only a few seconds before vanishing, leaving the witnesses startled and bewildered.

Among the countless tales of ghostly encounters at the Tenerife North Airport, one story, in particular, stands out due to the credibility of the witness and the specificity of the details.
In the late 1980s, an airport security officer named Luis was conducting a routine patrol of the terminal building late at night.

As he made his way through the deserted check-in area, he noticed a man standing by one of the counters. The man appeared to be in his 40s and was dressed in an outdated style of clothing that seemed out of place.

Taken aback by the man's presence, given that the terminal was supposed to be empty at that hour, Luis approached him and asked if he needed assistance. The man, however, did not respond. He simply stood there, staring blankly ahead. As Luis moved closer, he felt a sudden chill, despite the otherwise temperate conditions in the terminal.

The man remained silent, his gaze fixed on something unseen in the distance. Then, without warning, he turned towards Luis. His eyes, filled with an indescribable sadness, met Luis's, and he muttered a single, chilling word: "Fuego" – fire. As soon as the word left his lips, the man simply disappeared, leaving Luis alone in the dimly lit terminal.

Shaken by the encounter, Luis reported the incident to his superiors. It turned out that he wasn't the first to report such an encounter. Over the years, several other security officers had reported seeing the same man in the terminal late at night, always repeating the same haunting word: "Fuego".

The reports of these encounters sparked a wave of speculation among the airport staff. Some suggested that the man could be the ghost of one of the passengers who perished in the 1977 accident, forever trapped at the site of the tragedy. Others speculated that he might be a residual haunting, a kind of psychic imprint left behind by the intense emotions experienced during the accident.

Regardless of the truth behind these sightings, the fact remains that the Tenerife North Airport is a place that carries the weight of a profound tragedy. For many, it serves as a stark reminder of the fragility of life and the lasting impact of our actions.

The ghostly manifestations reported at the airport stand as testaments to the lingering echoes of that fateful day in March 1977. They speak to the enduring power of memory and the indelible mark that tragedy leaves behind, not only on the physical world but also on the realm of the unseen.

As we continue to navigate the bustling terminals and crowded runways of the world's airports, rushing to catch flights or awaiting the arrival of loved ones, it's worth pausing for a moment to acknowledge the stories, histories, and mysteries that permeate these spaces.

The tales contained within the pages of "Haunted Airports" serve to remind us that airports are more than just transitional spaces. They are complex tapestries woven with countless human stories, some of which continue to unfold even beyond the veil of mortality.

The story of the Tenerife North Airport and its ghostly inhabitants challenges us to look beyond the surface, to question our perceptions of reality, and to open our minds to the possibility that there may be more to this world than meets the eye. As we traverse these haunted airports, we are not just passengers or observers, but participants in an unfolding narrative that straddles the realms of the living and the dead, the seen and the unseen, the remembered and the forgotten.

Whether you are a believer in the supernatural or not, one thing is clear: the echoes of the past, both tragic and joyous, continue to reverberate in the present, reminding us of our shared humanity and our intrinsic connection to the world around us. Through these haunting tales, we are invited to explore the depths of our understanding, to question our assumptions, and to contemplate the enduring mysteries of existence.

As you turn the last page of this chapter, take a moment to

reflect on the stories you've read and the questions they've raised. Remember the tragic spirits of the Tenerife North Airport and the lessons they impart. And as you continue on your journey through "Haunted Airports", keep your mind open to the extraordinary possibilities that lie just beyond the realm of the ordinary. For, in the words of Shakespeare, "There are more things in heaven and earth, Horatio, than are dreamt of in your philosophy."

The Phantom Flight Attendants of Dallas/Fort Worth International Airport

Dallas/Fort Worth International Airport, sprawling over 17,207 acres and boasting its own postal code, is one of the busiest airports in the world. Serving over 75 million passengers annually and offering flights to more than 200 destinations, it's a hub of human activity, a place where people from all walks of life converge. But amidst the hustle and bustle, a spectral undercurrent persists, casting long, eerie shadows over the terminal halls. This chapter delves into the spine-chilling tales of the ghostly flight attendants that reputedly haunt the airport's terminals, their ethereal figures serving as an uncanny reminder of the airport's history and the lives intertwined with its operation.

The history of the Dallas/Fort Worth International Airport dates back to the early 1970s. Designed to supplant the region's smaller airports and accommodate the growing demand for air travel, the airport quickly grew in size and significance. With this rapid expansion came a multitude of stories and experiences, a rich tapestry of human emotion and activity. But not all of these stories ended when the flights touched down or when the airport lights dimmed for the night.

Over the years, numerous eyewitnesses have reported encounters with spectral figures dressed in flight attendant uniforms. These apparitions are often seen late at night, when the airport activity slows down, and the echoing sound of footsteps reverberates through the otherwise silent terminals.

One such account comes from a janitorial worker, Maria, who has been with the airport for over a decade. She recalls one winter night in 2005 when she was finishing her shift in Terminal C. As she was emptying the trash bins near the gate C14, she noticed a woman standing near the windows overlooking the runways. The woman was dressed in a vintage flight attendant uniform that Maria recognized as hailing from the 1970s or 80s, complete with a pillbox hat and a dark blue dress.

Perplexed by the woman's presence at this late hour and her outdated attire, Maria approached her to check if she needed assistance. As she neared, she noticed the woman's pale, almost translucent complexion, her gaze fixed on the planes outside. Maria called out to her, but the woman did not respond. She simply stood there, her expression sombre, as if lost in deep contemplation.

Feeling a surge of unease, Maria reached out to touch the woman's shoulder, but her hand met thin air. The woman had vanished as if she was never there. Maria stood there, her mind struggling to make sense of the inexplicable encounter.

Another chilling account comes from a night security guard, James, who has spent the better part of his career patrolling the sprawling airport. In his account, he speaks of a recurring encounter with a spectral figure near the old American Airlines Admirals Club in Terminal A. One night, while doing his usual rounds, he noticed a woman in a vintage flight attendant uniform, similar to the one described by Maria. The woman was walking down the hallway, her steps soundless, her figure barely discernible in the dim light. James called out to her, but she paid him no mind. She continued walking until she reached the end of the hallway and disappeared into thin air.

These uncanny encounters have not only been confined to airport staff. Travellers, too, have reported seeing spectral flight attendants. A frequent flyer, Rebecca, shared a harrowing encounter from a late-night layover at the airport. She was trying to catch some sleep in the sparsely populated Terminal B when she was woken up by the sound of a service trolley.

Opening her eyes, she saw a flight attendant pushing a trolley down the terminal. As the figure drew closer, Rebecca noticed the outdated uniform and the woman's ethereal, almost transparent figure. The apparition moved silently along the corridor, stopping occasionally as if to check on non-existent passengers. The spectral attendant then turned and disappeared into a wall, leaving a stunned Rebecca questioning her own senses.

These accounts, while chilling, seem to hint at a deeper narrative. The apparitions appear to be locked in a loop, repeating the same actions over and over again, as if bound by some unseen force to their former lives. There is a palpable sense of melancholy that pervades these encounters, a spectral residue of lives dedicated to service and care.

The airport administration, while not officially acknowledging these occurrences, has shown an understanding stance towards the tales. After all, these stories have become an intrinsic part of the airport's lore, a spectral undercurrent to the ceaseless tide of human activity. They serve as an uncanny reminder of the airport's history and its human aspect, the countless lives it has touched, and the stories etched into its very fabric.

Paranormal researchers, drawn to the airport by these accounts, speculate that these apparitions might be the manifestations of flight attendants who have had strong emotional ties to their jobs or had their lives cut tragically short. The outdated uniforms suggest that these spirits could belong to a bygone era, perhaps dating back to the early years of the airport's operations.

While the identities of these ghostly attendants remain shrouded in mystery, their stories continue to add an eerie depth to the overall human narrative of the Dallas/Fort Worth International Airport. They serve as spectral reminders of the airport's past, echoing through the terminals and chilling the spines of those who encounter them.

These tales of phantom flight attendants serve as the macabre counterpoint to the airport's otherwise mundane reality. They blur the boundaries between the living and the dead, the physical and the ethereal, stirring the depths of our understanding of reality.

Despite the fear and unease these apparitions inspire, there is also a sense of tragic beauty to these stories. They symbolise a spectral continuation of service, a commitment that transcends the boundaries of life and death. These phantom attendants, forever bound to the airport, continue their duties in death as they did in life, making Dallas/Fort Worth International Airport not just a hub of human activity, but a haunting crossroads of the earthly and the ethereal.

As we traverse the bustling terminals, catch our flights, or wait for our loved ones, we become a part of this narrative. We step into the spectral undercurrent, merging our stories with those of the phantom flight attendants. And as we do so, we add another layer to the haunting tapestry of the Dallas/Fort Worth International Airport, a tapestry woven from countless human stories, both of this world and the one beyond.

In the end, it is these stories that make the airport more than just a transportation hub. They transform it into a living, breathing entity, a place where human narratives converge, intertwine, and echo through time and space. These phantom flight attendants, in their spectral form, continue to serve, to care, and to exist, adding a haunting depth to our understanding of airports and the lives they touch.

The Haunted Hangar of Los Angeles International Airport

Los Angeles International Airport, fondly known as LAX, is a sprawling metropolis of steel, concrete, and glass. It's one of the busiest airports in the world, hosting nearly 90 million passengers annually. The airport stands as a testament to human achievement, embodying the relentless pace of modern life. Yet, hidden within its labyrinthine structure, in one particular hangar, lies a spectral world that stands in stark contrast to the airport's bustling reality.

The Hangar in question is Hangar 18. Sandwiched between the taxiways and runways, it's an unassuming structure, seemingly no different from the dozens of others that populate the airport grounds. Yet, over the years, the hangar has gained a reputation for being home to a host of paranormal activities, its eerie tales echoing in the hushed whispers of airport staff and travellers alike.

The tales of Hangar 18 are as varied as they are chilling. They range from unexplained noises to full-blown apparitions, each account adding a new layer to the hangar's eerie lore. Workers in and around the hangar report hearing strange sounds late at night, long after the airport activity slows down. The clanging of tools, the rustling of chains, and the muffled voices, all emanating from an empty, locked hangar.

One notable account comes from a mechanic named Carl. He recalls working late one night on an aircraft parked near Hangar 18. As he worked, he started hearing faint noises coming from the hangar. Thinking it was one of his colleagues pulling a prank, he decided to investigate. As he approached the hangar, the noises grew louder, morphing into what sounded like a heated argument between several people. The hangar door was locked, and peering through the small window, he could see that the hangar was empty. Yet the sounds continued, growing in intensity before abruptly stopping, leaving Carl standing in the eerie silence, his heart pounding in his chest.

Another account comes from a night security guard named Rosa. While patrolling the airport grounds one night, she noticed a figure standing in the doorway of Hangar 18. The figure, a man dressed in an old-fashioned pilot's uniform, stood there silently, staring at the runways. Rosa called out to him, but the man didn't respond. He simply stood there, his figure illuminated by the hangar lights, before slowly fading away, leaving an empty doorway and a stunned Rosa behind.

Travellers, too, have reported strange occurrences around Hangar 18. One frequent flyer, a businessman named Richard, recalls waiting for his flight in the nearby terminal. As he gazed out the window at the airport grounds, his eyes were drawn to Hangar 18. In the dim light, he could see a group of figures moving around the hangar, loading and unloading an invisible plane. He watched in disbelief as the spectral crew carried out their duties, their translucent figures glowing in the moonlight. Then, as suddenly as they appeared, they vanished, leaving Richard questioning his own senses.

The tales of Hangar 18 are not confined to the visual or auditory. Many who have ventured close to the hangar speak of an inexplicable chill that pervades the area, a chill that seeps into the bones despite the warm Californian weather. Others speak of an uncanny sense of being watched, of invisible eyes tracking their every move.

The eerie tales of Hangar 18 have added a spectral undercurrent to the otherwise mundane reality of LAX. They serve as a chilling reminder of the airport's history and the lives intertwined with its operation. The spectral crew continues to carry out their duties, forever bound to the airport, their stories echoing in the hushed whispers and stunned silences of those who encounter them.

As the tales of Hangar 18 ripple through the airport community, they do more than just raise the hair on the back of the neck; they add a layer of depth to the human narrative of LAX. They remind us that the airport is not just a hub of human activity but a repository of countless stories, both of this world and beyond.

But who are these spectral figures that inhabit Hangar 18? What ties them to the hangar, compelling them to carry out their duties long after their earthly existence has ceased? These questions remain unanswered, adding to the intrigue and mystery of Hangar 18. Some speculate that these apparitions are the spirits of crew members who lost their lives in air accidents over the years, their spirits tied to the place of their untimely demise. Others posit that they are echoes of a bygone era, their residual energy imprinted on the hangar due to some strong emotional event.

As we delve deeper into the eerie tales of Hangar 18, we come to realise that these stories are more than just hair-raising ghost tales; they are narratives of human lives, of individuals who dedicated their lives to the service of others. They are the echoes of the past resonating in the present, bridging the gap between the living and the dead.

These tales also underscore the power of belief and the persistence of memory. They remind us that stories, even ghostly ones, are an integral part of our collective consciousness, their power residing not just in their ability to thrill and chill, but also in their capacity to connect us with our past. The spectral crew of Hangar 18, in their ghostly form, continue to serve, to exist, to be a part of the narrative, weaving a haunting tale of duty, commitment, and perseverance.

As we traverse the bustling terminals of LAX, we become a part of this narrative, our stories merging with those of the spectral crew. And as we do so, we add another layer to the haunting tapestry of LAX, a tapestry woven from countless human stories, both of this world and the next.

In the end, these tales transform LAX from a mere transportation hub to a living, breathing entity, a place where human narratives converge, intertwine, and echo through time and space. The haunted Hangar 18 stands as a spectral monument to these narratives, its eerie tales a testament to the indomitable human spirit and its capacity to resonate beyond the confines of life and death.

The Lost Souls of Charles de Gaulle Airport

Charles de Gaulle Airport, sprawling across the outskirts of Paris, is renowned as a marvel of modern architecture and a bustling hub of global connectivity. Its sheer scale and the ceaseless thrum of human activity often belies the less tangible, more spectral narratives that echo in its seemingly endless corridors. It is in these hidden narratives that we find the lost souls of Charles de Gaulle Airport, spectral figures that remain forever tethered to the airport, their presence a haunting reminder of the airport's past.

Charles de Gaulle Airport's history is as captivating as it is complex. Named after the former French president, it opened its doors in 1974 with the vision of being a futuristic model for airports worldwide. The airport's radial design, inspired by an octopus, was a departure from the linear layouts of traditional airports, a testament to innovation and architectural prowess. But it is not this history that forms the crux of our exploration. Rather, it is the tales of lost souls, of spectral figures forever trapped in its confines, that draw our attention.

The stories vary, each more chilling than the last. From the spectre of a man in an outdated airline uniform roaming the terminals to the soft echoes of a woman's laughter in the quiet corners of the airport, these tales have long been whispered among airport staff and frequent travellers. However, the most recurring narrative revolves around the apparitions of passengers who seem perpetually lost, wandering aimlessly, their spectral forms adding a ghostly layer to the airport's physical dimensions.

One such tale involves a woman, dressed in early 20th-century attire, often seen in Terminal 1. Described as being in her mid-thirties, she is said to appear solid, not ethereal like most apparitions. Witnesses recount how she seems perpetually confused, often seen staring at the flight information boards, her lips moving as if trying to figure out her flight. It's as if she's stuck in a loop, repeating the same actions over and over again.

Then there is the tale of a young boy often seen near the

airport's old control tower. Described as no older than ten, he is often spotted staring out at the runways, his eyes filled with longing. Witnesses often recall an overwhelming sense of sadness when they spot him, a shared melancholy that seems to hang in the air long after he has vanished.

Perhaps the most spine-chilling tale is that of a group of passengers seen on the anniversary of a plane crash that occurred in the 1980s. Witnesses have reported seeing a group of people, their clothes reflecting the fashion of the era, waiting near a departure gate that no longer exists. They appear as solid as living people, often causing confusion among those who see them. As the story goes, they are usually seen early in the morning, and they disappear the moment the clock strikes the hour of the ill-fated flight's departure.

These stories, while chilling, paint a portrait of an airport that is more than just a hub of human activity. They reveal an airport that exists in multiple dimensions, where the living and the dead coexist, their narratives interweaving to form the airport's unique tapestry.

As these tales of the lost souls of Charles de Gaulle Airport are shared, they transform the airport from a mere physical space into a narrative landscape, a place imbued with stories that transcend the boundaries of life and death. They remind us that the airport is more than just a symbol of human endeavour and connectivity. It is a repository of human experiences, of stories that echo in its corridors, a place where past and present merge in a haunting symphony.

In the end, these tales remind us that airports, in their unique ways, are not just about departures and arrivals in a physical sense, but also symbolise the constant ebb and flow of human experiences, memories, and emotions. They embody the essence of our shared humanity, a place where joy, sorrow, longing, and even the spectral, coexist. The tales of the lost souls of Charles de Gaulle Airport remind us that sometimes, those who pass through these spaces leave behind more than just footprints. They leave echoes of their presence, stories that continue to resonate, transforming these hubs of human activity into portals of the extraordinary. Through these tales, the airport sheds its concrete and steel exterior, revealing a soul that is as complex, haunting, and human as the stories it cradles.

The Ghostly Soldiers of Okinawa's Naha Airport

Steeped in history, the Naha Airport in Okinawa, Japan, serves as a tangible reminder of the city's turbulent past. An island marked by the indelible scars of war, Okinawa was the site of one of World War II's most brutal and decisive battles. Today, the island's main airport, Naha, is known not just for its bustling terminals and modern facilities, but for its spectral inhabitants – the ghostly soldiers who are believed to still roam its premises.

Naha Airport's history is inextricably linked with the Second World War. In the early 1940s, the airport was a key military base for the Japanese, serving as a launchpad for their aerial operations. However, its strategic significance made it a prime target for the Allies, and in 1945, during the Battle of Okinawa, the airport was seized and occupied by American forces. The brutal conflict claimed the lives of over 100,000 Japanese soldiers, many of whom were stationed at or around Naha Airport.

These traumatic events etched themselves deeply into the fabric of Okinawa's history, leaving a residue of pain, loss, and fear that has endured for decades. It is within this context that the tales of the ghostly soldiers of Naha Airport have taken root, casting a spectral shadow over the otherwise ordinary hustle and bustle of the modern airport.

One of the most frequently recounted sightings is that of the ghostly platoon. Airport staff and visitors alike report seeing a spectral group of Japanese soldiers in full wartime attire, marching in formation across the tarmac, as if eternally bound to their military duties. These apparitions are often seen in the early hours of the morning, fading away as the first light of day breaks.

Other reports tell of disembodied voices speaking in hushed tones, echoing through the airport's halls and corridors in the dead of night. The voices, speaking in old dialects of Japanese, are said to utter cryptic orders and pleas for help, casting an eerie pall over the airport's otherwise mundane nocturnal soundscape.

Yet another chilling tale involves the ghostly pilot. Numerous airport workers have reported sightings of a spectral figure, clad in a pilot's uniform from the era of the Second World War, appearing in and around the hangars. These eyewitnesses describe the apparition as seemingly solid and real, only to disappear when approached. The figure is often seen inspecting the planes, as if preparing for a mission that will never come.

In the face of such eerie occurrences, the airport authorities have taken the reports seriously. Rituals and prayers have been performed to appease the restless spirits, and the airport has even invited spiritualists and paranormal experts to investigate the phenomenon. Yet, despite these efforts, the sightings and strange happenings continue unabated, as if the ghostly soldiers are forever trapped in their wartime roles, unable to find peace.

In attempting to understand these spectral manifestations, it's important to consider the cultural context. In Japan, the concept of "yūrei," or ghosts, is deeply ingrained in the national psyche. Japanese folklore is filled with tales of yūrei who linger in the physical world due to unresolved issues or intense emotions, such as anger, sorrow, or regret. The ghosts of Naha Airport could very well be viewed through this cultural lens, as soldiers unable to move on due to the trauma and violent circumstances of their deaths.

Moreover, the ghosts of Naha Airport are not just a source of fear and intrigue, but also poignant reminders of the island's past. The spectral soldiers, forever bound to their duty, serve as silent witnesses to the devastating toll of war, embodying a chilling testament to the countless lives that were abruptly ended and forever altered by the conflict. They stand as spectral sentinels, their presence a spectral echo of a time marked by profound suffering and loss.

The ghostly soldiers of Naha Airport also contribute to a broader conversation about the interaction of past and present, memory and reality. Airports, as sites of transient passage, are typically associated with the here and now, with the relentless forward march of time. Yet, in Naha Airport, the past refuses to be relegated to the annals of history. Instead, it lingers, manifesting in the form of spectral soldiers who roam the airport's tarmac and hangars, a haunting reminder of the island's war-torn past.

The spectral phenomena at Naha Airport challenge our conventional understanding of space and time. Here, the airport serves not just as a physical gateway connecting different geographical locations, but also as a temporal portal where the past and the present collide in the most unexpected ways. The spectral soldiers, in their ghostly attire, marching in formation or inspecting the planes, disrupt the linear progression of time, reminding us that the past is not always something that can be neatly tucked away. It seeps into the present, revealing itself in the most unexpected ways, challenging us to reassess our understanding of history, memory, and the residual impact of past events on our present reality.

It also forces us to consider the human cost of war. The spectral soldiers of Naha Airport, in their ceaseless haunting, draw attention to the lives cut short, the dreams unfulfilled, and the families torn apart by the devastation of conflict. They stand as a chilling reminder of the toll of war, their ghostly presence a haunting testament to the suffering and sacrifice endured by so many during those dark times.

The ghostly soldiers of Naha Airport serve as a stark reminder of the island's past, of the sacrifices made and lives lost during one of history's most brutal conflicts. They are a spectral echo of a time of war, their presence a haunting testament to the airport's history, imbuing it with a ghostly aura that is felt by all who visit.

While the bustling activity of the airport continues, the spectral soldiers of Naha Airport serve as a chilling reminder that beneath the veneer of modernity, the echoes of the past continue to resonate. Their haunting presence, eternally bound to the airport, serves as a poignant symbol of the island's history, a spectral embodiment of the trauma and loss etched into Okinawa's collective memory.

The chilling tales of the ghostly soldiers of Naha Airport give us pause, inviting us to reflect on the enduring impact of the past, the weight of memory, and the intertwining of the physical and spiritual worlds. They prompt us to consider the ways in which history continues to echo in our present, subtly shaping our perception of the world around us. As we traverse the modern, bustling terminals of Naha Airport, we are reminded of the spectral soldiers who continue to roam its premises, a haunting reminder of a past that continues to reverberate in the present.

The Eerie Presence at Sydney's Kingsford Smith Airport

Australia's largest and busiest airport, Sydney's Kingsford Smith Airport, is known for more than just its bustling terminals, busy runways, and the millions of passengers who pass through its gates annually. It's also known for something far more eerie, something that lurks in the shadows of an abandoned hangar. It's here where stories have been spun, tales whispered amongst airport staff and travellers alike, of a spectral figure that haunts the premises.

Kingsford Smith Airport's history extends back to the early 20th century, when it was first established as an airfield in 1920. Named after Sir Charles Kingsford Smith, a pioneer in Australian aviation, the airport quickly grew in size and significance over the decades, transforming into the international hub it is today. Yet, amidst its modern advancements and ceaseless activity, a piece of its past has seemingly refused to fade away, etching itself into the annals of the airport's eerie lore.

The stories revolve around Hangar 85, a disused structure that stands somewhat removed from the main facilities of the airport. Originally built during the Second World War, Hangar 85 served as an important base for military aircraft during the tumultuous years of the conflict. It was in this very hangar, saturated with the energy of wartime urgency and fear, that the first sightings of the spectral figure were reported.

Over the years, numerous accounts have emerged of a shadowy figure seen wandering around the hangar and its vicinity, particularly during the early morning hours or late at night. Described as a man dressed in a pilot's uniform from the mid-20th century, the figure is said to exude an aura of melancholy, forever trapped in a time and place he can't escape.

Airport staff who have had the misfortune of crossing paths with this spectral entity speak of a sudden chill in the air, an inexplicable feeling of sadness, and a sense of being watched. Some have even reported hearing the faint sound of an old-time radio broadcast, the kind used by pilots and air traffic controllers in the era of the Second World War.

Another chilling tale from Hangar 85 involves an old, decommissioned aircraft that's been stored there for decades. Several airport staff members have reported seeing the spectral pilot inside the aircraft's cockpit, looking out over the runway with a pensive expression. According to these accounts, the figure appears solid, and his presence is so strong that many have initially mistaken him for a living person, only to watch in shock as he vanishes before their eyes.

The spectral figure haunting Hangar 85 is widely believed to be the ghost of a pilot who lost his life during the Second World War. Although no specific records exist to conclusively link the haunting to a particular individual, the theory aligns with the nature of the apparition and the era from which it appears to hail. The ghostly pilot, forever donned in his uniform, his spirit tethered to the vintage aircraft and the hangar, seems to be a residual echo of the airport's wartime past.

The stories of the ghostly pilot of Kingsford Smith Airport serve as a poignant reminder of the airport's vibrant history, a history that is seemingly so powerful that it continues to make its presence felt in the most unexpected ways. The spectral pilot, forever bound to the airport and the hangar that once teemed with wartime urgency, stands as a symbol of a time when the world was in turmoil and the airport served as a critical node in the theatre of war. His eternal presence speaks to the enduring human connection to places of significance and the powerful emotional imprints left behind by historical events.

The spectral figure's haunting presence also challenges the conventional notion of airports as transient, non-place spaces. The ghostly pilot, eternally bound to Hangar 85, transforms the airport from a place of transitory passage to a site of historical memory and emotional resonance. He disrupts the fast-paced, forward-looking momentum of airport dynamics, compelling us to pause, to look back, and to remember.

The eerie encounters at Sydney's Kingsford Smith Airport remind us that the past is never truly gone, that it lingers and echoes in the corners of our present existence. The spectral pilot of Hangar 85 stands as a testament to the past's enduring resonance, a chilling embodiment of a bygone era that refuses to be forgotten.

In the grand scheme of things, the stories of the ghostly pilot are more than just tales of a haunted airport. They offer a glimpse into the past, a reflection of the wartime history of Kingsford Smith Airport, and a spectral narrative of a pilot who, even in death, continues to patrol his post, bound to the aircraft he once navigated and the hangar he once called home.

As we conclude this chapter, we leave you with a sense of the profound impact that history can have on a place, and how it can manifest itself in the most unexpected ways. The spectral figure of the pilot, haunting Hangar 85, serves as a poignant reminder of the airport's past, a haunting echo of the fears, hopes, and sacrifices of an era marked by global conflict.

The eerie presence at Sydney's Kingsford Smith Airport, particularly in the abandoned Hangar 85, is a chilling testament to the airport's vibrant history and the powerful human narratives that have unfolded within its precincts. It's a reminder that every place, even an airport bustling with activity, has a story to tell, a history to share, and sometimes, a ghost to reveal.

The Haunting of Atlanta's Hartsfield-Jackson International Airport

The Atlanta Hartsfield-Jackson International Airport, familiarly known as Atlanta's airport, is a hive of ceaseless activity, a bustling testament to human ingenuity and the relentless march of progress. Officially designated as the world's busiest airport in terms of passenger traffic, it is a marvel of modern transportation, handling more than 200,000 passengers daily, and offering flights to over 150 domestic and 70 international destinations. However, beneath the veneer of its modernity and efficiency, the airport harbours a darker, more mysterious side. It is an arena where spectral apparitions roam the terminals, where inexplicable cold spots appear out of nowhere, and where disembodied voices echo in the stillness of the night.

The airport's history stretches back to the early 20th century, a time when aviation was in its infancy. The site where the airport now stands was originally a racetrack, which was converted into an airfield in the 1920s. As the years passed, the airport expanded and modernised, transforming into the vast, sprawling complex we see today. Yet, even as the airport evolved, whispers of its haunted past persisted, passed down from generation to generation of airport staff and frequent travellers.

One of the most pervasive tales is that of a ghostly woman who has been spotted in the terminals late at night. Clad in a 1940s-era dress, she is said to glide silently along the corridors, her pale face expressionless and her eyes devoid of life. She never interacts with the living, appearing lost in her own world. Over the years, numerous airport employees and passengers have reported encountering this spectral figure, often describing a sudden drop in temperature and a feeling of profound sadness accompanying her presence.

The identity of this spectral woman is the subject of much speculation. Some believe she is the ghost of a passenger who died in one of the many plane crashes that have occurred in the airport's vicinity over the years. Others speculate that she was a former airport employee who met a tragic end. Whatever her origins, her story serves as a haunting reminder of the airport's long and eventful history, a history that continues to echo in its modern corridors.

Another spectral figure often sighted at the airport is that of a man dressed in a pilot's uniform. This apparition has been seen wandering around the airport's tarmac, appearing to carry out pre-flight checks on non-existent planes. The apparition is always seen alone, seemingly oblivious to the bustling activity around him. Eyewitnesses often report a feeling of intense loneliness and despair emanating from the spectral pilot. His identity, like the ghostly woman's, remains a mystery, but his presence is a chilling testament to the countless pilots who have passed through the airport over the decades.

In addition to these apparitions, there are numerous reports of other eerie phenomena at the airport. Disembodied voices have been heard echoing through the terminals late at night when the airport is at its quietest. These voices, sometimes male, sometimes female, are often heard speaking in hushed, urgent tones, as if carrying out a conversation. No source for these voices has ever been found, adding to the airport's enigmatic allure.

Similarly, inexplicable cold spots have been experienced in various parts of the airport. These sudden drops in temperature, which occur without any discernible reason, have been known to send shivers down the spines of even the most seasoned airport staff. There are areas within the airport, otherwise bustling and full of life during the day, that are avoided late at night due to the unnatural chill that pervades the air.

Along with these chilling accounts, stories of inexplicable malfunctions of electronic equipment add to the eerie reputation of Atlanta's Hartsfield-Jackson International Airport. There are tales of lights flickering without cause, of radios emitting static or strange voices, of automatic doors opening and closing on their own accord. These phenomena often occur in the dead of night, when the airport is at its quietest, contributing to the unsettling atmosphere.

Yet, it's not just the physical phenomena that lends credence to the haunted reputation of Atlanta's airport. There are numerous accounts from airport staff and passengers alike, who report feeling an inexplicable sense of dread or unease in certain parts of the airport. This feeling, often described as a heavy, oppressive sensation, has been known to overwhelm even the most rational and sceptical individuals.

The testimonies of those who have encountered these spectral figures and experienced these eerie phenomena paint a vivid picture of an airport teeming with unseen presences. These accounts, drawn from a diverse group of individuals, ranging from seasoned pilots and air traffic controllers to weary travellers, underscore the pervasiveness of the airport's haunted reputation.

The airport, in many ways, serves as a microcosm of human life. It is a place of hellos and goodbyes, of joyous reunions and tearful departures, of hopes, dreams, and farewells. The countless emotions that have been experienced within its walls have, over time, imbued the airport with a certain energy, an energy that, some believe, has given rise to its spectral inhabitants.

"Haunted Airports" invites you on a journey into the world of the supernatural that exists parallel to our own, a world that is often overlooked amid the hustle and bustle of daily life. The stories of Atlanta's Hartsfield-Jackson International Airport serve as a potent reminder that, even in places teeming with life and activity, there are hidden layers of mystery and intrigue that lie beneath the surface, waiting to be explored.

The Wandering Spirits of Newark Liberty International Airport

Newark Liberty International Airport, situated in the state of New Jersey, is one of the primary airports serving the U.S. metropolitan area of New York City. Among the oldest airports in the United States, Newark Liberty International has a rich history that dates back to its opening on October 1, 1928. It was the first major airport in the metropolitan area, beating out LaGuardia and John F. Kennedy airports by a number of years.

During its nine decades of operation, Newark Liberty International Airport has seen the passage of millions of travellers, the evolution of aviation technology, and its fair share of historical events. It served as the departure point for the first transatlantic commercial flight, helmed by Amelia Earhart in

1939, and has since grown to become a major hub for United Airlines and a host of other domestic and international carriers.

Yet, as with any place that has been a crossroads of human activity for so long, there are layers to Newark Liberty International that go beyond the visible. Beneath the hum of jet engines, the bustle of passengers, and the steady rhythm of arrivals and departures, whispers of a different kind of history can be heard. A history not recorded in books or newspapers, but passed down through hushed conversations and uneasy glances. It is a history of inexplicable phenomena and haunting apparitions, of eerie incidents that defy rational explanation.

One of the most enduring tales is that of a spectral figure in a pilot's uniform. Staff working the late-night shift have reported encounters with this apparition in the older sections of the airport, where reminders of past eras can still be seen in the architecture and decor. He's most often described as a man in his mid-30s, dressed in the style of the 1940s, complete with a leather bomber jacket and a cap emblazoned with an airline insignia that no longer exists.

This spectral pilot doesn't engage with the living or cause any disturbance. He merely wanders the empty corridors and dimly lit corners of the airport, a silent spectre seemingly lost in time. On the rare occasion when a staff member has gathered the courage to approach him, he disappears into thin air, leaving behind a chill that has nothing to do with the airport's air conditioning.

Then there is the young woman who has been seen in the main terminal building, usually in the late hours of the night. Witnesses describe her as being in her early 20s, dressed in an outfit that would have been fashionable in the mid-20th century. She is often seen sitting alone, her attention fixed on the departure screens, even when no flights are scheduled. Despite her spectral nature, there is a palpable sense of sadness that surrounds her, a melancholy that has moved more than one onlooker to tears. As with the pilot, any attempt to approach or interact with her results in her disappearing.

In addition to these apparitions, there are numerous accounts of unexplained phenomena that add to Newark Liberty International's haunted reputation. Lights flicker inexplicably, voices echo in otherwise empty halls, and doors open and close of their own volition. Baggage handlers have reported hearing the sound of footsteps behind them, only to turn around and find no one there. And on more than one occasion, a flight crew preparing for a late-night departure has reported an unseen presence in the cockpit.

These tales of the supernatural aren't limited to the airport's staff. Passengers, too, have reported encounters that defy explanation. Some speak of feeling an unseen hand on their shoulder, while others tell of hearing whispered voices in an otherwise quiet terminal. A few have even claimed to have seen the spectral pilot or the forlorn young woman, their own encounters adding to the growing body of ghostly lore surrounding the airport.

One particular tale that has gained traction involves a group of travellers waiting for a red-eye flight. As the story goes, they noticed an elderly gentleman sitting alone, his eyes closed as if in deep thought. His dress was noticeably out of place, resembling the attire of the early 20th century. Despite the late hour and the sparse crowd, no one approached the man, attributing his presence to the eccentricities one often witnesses during late-night travels.

As their flight time approached, the passengers gathered their belongings and prepared to board. The elderly man remained seated, however, prompting a kind-hearted traveller to inform him of the impending departure. On approaching the man, the traveller was startled to find the seat empty, the impression of a person still visible on the cushion. The sudden chill and the prickling sense of unease were enough to convince the traveller that they had just experienced an encounter with the supernatural.

While not everyone who passes through Newark Liberty International experiences these supernatural occurrences, the tales persist, passed along by those who have had their own brush with the inexplicable. The spectral pilot continues his lonely patrol, the young woman waits eternally for a flight that will never come, and the unseen presences continue to make themselves known in ways that chill and bewilder.

It's easy to dismiss these stories as mere figments of imagination, products of weary minds in the dreary hours of the night. But the consistency of these tales, the sincerity of those who share them, and the specific details that remain unchanged over years lend a certain weight to the ghostly lore of Newark Liberty International Airport.

The Haunted Halls of Berlin-Tegel Airport

Berlin-Tegel Airport, once known as Otto Lilienthal Airport, was more than an architectural marvel or an important hub for international flights. It was a place whose walls echoed with the whispers of history, bearing the scars of a divided city and the silent hopes of thousands who passed through its gates. Now silent and devoid of the sounds of roaring jet engines, this airport has seen more than just the comings and goings of travellers. It has witnessed an array of supernatural occurrences that continue to baffle and terrify even after its closure in 2020.

One of the most enduring tales from Berlin-Tegel involves a spectral figure known as "The Watcher." Airport staff, security personnel, and passengers alike reported seeing an individual in a Cold War-era uniform standing quietly in the terminal. Hans, a janitor who worked at the airport for over 20 years, recalls his first encounter with this apparition. "I was cleaning late at night when I noticed a man standing near the departure gate," he said. "He was dressed in an old uniform, just watching the empty chairs. I called out to him, thinking he was a passenger who'd lost his way, but he just vanished right in front of my eyes."

"The Watcher" wasn't the only ghostly figure reported at the airport. The labyrinthine network of tunnels beneath the airport, originally designed for baggage transport and maintenance, was also a hotbed for eerie encounters. Staff members reported hearing whispered voices, the clanking of old machinery, and an inexplicable chill in certain spots. Stefan, a maintenance worker, reported encountering a group of spectral figures huddled together, appearing terrified. "They were dressed in old-fashioned clothes, huddled like they were hiding from something," Stefan said. "When they noticed me, they faded away. It was as if they were still living the fear of being discovered."

The stories weren't just confined to the ground level. The control tower at Berlin-Tegel was another focal point for supernatural occurrences. Numerous air traffic controllers reported receiving radio transmissions filled with static and what sounded like garbled German. Michael, a former air traffic controller, often received these transmissions during the graveyard shift. "I'd be monitoring the frequencies when suddenly, I'd get a transmission on a channel that we never used. It was always the same—static and then a voice speaking German. It sounded urgent, like a distress call, but it was too garbled to make out the words."

Even the terminal buildings, with their stark, modernist architecture, had their share of eerie incidents. Travellers often reported feeling watched or followed, especially during the late hours of the night. Emma, a frequent traveller through Berlin-Tegel, once shared her unnerving experience. "I was walking down the corridor towards the exit when I felt a tap on my shoulder. I turned around, expecting to see another passenger, but there was no one there. It felt so real, I couldn't believe I was alone."

As the sun set on Berlin-Tegel's operational life, the stories of ghostly encounters did not fade away. Instead, they became a part of the airport's legacy, a spectral history that lived on in the memories of those who had experienced it. These tales continue to colour the narrative of Berlin-Tegel, serving as chilling reminders of an era marked by political tension and human drama.

These stories serve as more than spine-chilling anecdotes—they are part of the rich tapestry of Berlin-Tegel's history. They remind us that places, much like people, carry their past with them, bearing silent witness to the events that have shaped them. And in spaces like Berlin-Tegel, these echoes of the past can manifest in truly haunting ways, leaving an indelible mark on those who encounter them.

A more recent account comes from a group of construction workers who were tasked with some renovations in the airport after its closure. Lead contractor, Klaus, recalls their eerie experience. "We were in the old terminal building, replacing some old fixtures. It was late, and the place was deserted. Suddenly, we heard a sound like a crowd—people talking, suitcases rolling, announcements over the PA system. But when we went to check, there was nothing. It was like the airport had come back to life for a few minutes."

In a similar vein, a security team that patrolled the decommissioned airport reported regular disturbances that defied explanation. Their supervisor, a stern, pragmatic man named Friedrich, was initially sceptical about the tales of apparitions and unexplained noises. However, he soon found himself unable to deny the strange occurrences. During one of his night patrols, Friedrich came across a little girl crying in one of the empty baggage claim areas. As he approached her to offer help, she disappeared right before his eyes, leaving behind only the echoing sound of her sobs.

Perhaps one of the most chilling accounts comes from a group of urban explorers who ventured into the airport in 2021. Drawn by the eerie allure of the abandoned structures, they came equipped with cameras, hoping to document their exploration. What they weren't prepared for was an encounter with the inexplicable. As they ventured deeper into the terminal, their equipment started malfunctioning. Batteries drained, lights flickered, and finally, their camera captured what appeared to be a figure in a pilot's uniform, standing in a doorway that led to an old hangar. The figure stood still for a moment before turning and walking away, disappearing into thin air.

The tales of Berlin-Tegel are a fascinating blend of history and mystery, a testament to the airport's rich past and its enduring legacy. From the apparition of "The Watcher" to the cries of the little girl lost in the baggage claim, the stories continue to enthral and terrify, adding a spectral dimension to the airport's Cold War history.

Even now, with the airport's doors closed to travellers, the tales of eerie encounters and phantom figures persist. The deserted halls, silent runways, and vacant control towers of Berlin-Tegel Airport continue to serve as the backdrop for spectral narratives, whispered accounts of unexplained phenomena, and chilling encounters. They are a testament to the indelible impressions left by history and the enduring power of stories that dare to venture into the realm of the inexplicable.

Though no longer a hub of human activity, Berlin-Tegel Airport remains a bustling hub for the spectral, the eerie, and the unexplained. Its empty corridors and vacant lounges are inhabited by more than just memories—they bear silent witness to the spectral residue of a bygone era, a haunting echo of the past that continues to resonate in the silence of the present.

The Phantom Flight of Amsterdam's Schiphol Airport

As you turn the page to Chapter 15, prepare yourself to delve into the mysterious tales surrounding Amsterdam's Schiphol Airport. Renowned as one of the busiest airports in the world, Schiphol has a rich history that dates back to its establishment in 1916 as a military airbase. Over the decades, it has witnessed the comings and goings of millions of travellers, all the while harbouring an enigmatic presence that has captivated the imaginations of many. This chapter unfolds the airport's history interwoven with the chilling tale of a spectral aircraft – a phantom flight that has been the subject of numerous eyewitness accounts and continues to fuel the aura of mystery that envelopes the airport.

Schiphol Airport, located 9 kilometres southwest of Amsterdam, has been at the heart of the city's development and growth. Its strategic location made it a vital hub during World War II, when it was expanded and used by the Germans. Post-war, Schiphol underwent significant transformation, quickly becoming a major player in global aviation. With its state-of-the-art facilities and distinctive architecture, it's a symbol of Dutch innovation and progress. Yet, beneath this vibrant facade of modernity and efficiency, Schiphol harbours a spectral presence that has long been a part of its folklore.

The story of Schiphol's phantom flight begins with a tragic incident during World War II. On a cold November night in 1943, a British bomber, the Avro Lancaster, was returning from a mission over Berlin. Heavily damaged by anti-aircraft fire, the aircraft was struggling to stay airborne. The crew, desperate to land, aimed for the lights of what they thought was an airfield. Unfortunately, it turned out to be the Schiphol Airport, then under German control. The aircraft was shot down, tragically ending the lives of the crew on board.

In the years following this tragic event, there have been consistent reports from airport staff, pilots, and even passengers about an eerie phenomenon: the sighting of a phantom aircraft resembling the Avro Lancaster. These encounters often occur on foggy nights, when visibility is low. Eyewitnesses report seeing the ghostly plane flying perilously low, its engines sputtering, as if in trouble. Air traffic controllers, despite hearing the distressed engine sounds, find no trace of the plane on their radar. Then, just as it appears to be on a collision course with the runway, the phantom plane vanishes.

One of the most notable accounts comes from a veteran pilot, Jan Van Der Kolk, who had been flying for KLM Royal Dutch Airlines for over 30 years. In the winter of 1985, Van Der Kolk was preparing for a routine flight to London when he saw the phantom Lancaster. "It was just past midnight, and a thick fog had settled over the airport," he recalls. "As I was carrying out the pre-flight checks, I noticed a plane approaching the runway at an unusually low altitude. It was an old model, like those used during the war, and it looked like it was in trouble. I alerted the tower, but they said there were no such flights scheduled. I watched as the plane descended, bracing myself for the crash. But then, it just...disappeared. It was there one moment and gone the next. It was like nothing I'd ever seen."

Airport ground staff have also reported strange experiences. One such tale comes from a maintenance worker, Els Van Dam, who has been working night shifts at Schiphol for over a decade. "I was out near the runway, fixing a faulty light," she narrates. "Suddenly, I heard the sound of a plane in distress. I looked up and saw the outline of an aircraft descending through the fog. It was a haunting sight, the old plane fighting to stay in the air, its engines sputtering and smoking. It was heading straight for the runway, but there was no scheduled landing at that time. I froze, unsure of what to do. And then, just as it was about to crash, it vanished into thin air. The noise, the smoke, everything disappeared. I was left standing there, alone in the fog, wondering if I'd imagined the whole thing."

Intriguingly, it's not just those who work at the airport who have reported sightings of the phantom flight. Travellers, too, have been privy to this spectral occurrence. One such account comes from Anna Bakker, a frequent flyer who was waiting for her late-night flight to Stockholm. "I was looking out of the terminal window when I saw an old-fashioned plane descending towards the runway," she says. "It looked like it was struggling to land, its engines making a dreadful noise. I remember feeling a sense of dread, convinced I was about to witness a terrible accident. But then, just as it was about to hit the ground, it disappeared. I blinked, thinking my eyes were playing tricks on me. But when I looked around, I saw that others had seen it too. We exchanged stunned glances, all of us speechless."

These eerie encounters have been the subject of much speculation and intrigue. Many believe that the phantom plane is the ghost of the ill-fated Avro Lancaster, its crew doomed to repeat their final moments over and over again. Others argue that it's a residual haunting, a replay of the past imprinted in the fabric of the place due to the intense emotions and energy released during the tragic event.

Despite the lack of concrete evidence to validate these ghostly sightings, the frequency of the reports and the credibility of the witnesses make it a tale hard to dismiss. The story of the phantom flight of Schiphol Airport continues to captivate those who hear it, adding an eerie layer to the airport's rich tapestry of history.

Schiphol, with its sleek architecture and bustling terminals, stands as a testament to human ingenuity and the rapid strides of technological progress. Yet, the phantom flight serves as a chilling reminder of its tumultuous past and the tragic losses endured during the war. As you walk through the modern terminals of Schiphol Airport, you can't help but sense the echoes of the past lingering in the air, whispers of a spectral plane forever trapped in its final, fatal descent.

This eerie tale from Amsterdam's Schiphol Airport is yet another chilling account that adds to the growing collection of ghostly narratives in our exploration of haunted airports. It brings to the fore the mystery and intrigue that shroud these seemingly ordinary places, reminding us that sometimes, the most extraordinary stories are hidden in plain sight, waiting to be discovered.

The tale of Schiphol's phantom flight invites us to question the boundaries of our understanding and to consider the possibility that the past may bleed into the present in ways we can't explain. It's a tale that underscores the power of memory and the enduring impact of tragedy, a story that continues to reverberate through the halls of one of the world's busiest airports.

The phantom flight of Amsterdam's Schiphol Airport serves as a stark reminder that places, like people, carry their past with them.

The Unexplained Happenings at Toronto Pearson International Airport

Chapter 16 of "Haunted Airports" takes us across the Atlantic to the bustling city of Toronto, Canada, home to one of the largest and busiest airports in North America: the Toronto Pearson International Airport. Named after the fourteenth Prime Minister of Canada, Lester B. Pearson, the airport is a hub of ceaseless activity, teeming with travellers from around the world. Yet, beneath the veneer of this bustling metropolis of transit, lie tales of eerie occurrences and unexplained phenomena that have left even the most grounded individuals unnerved.

Toronto Pearson International Airport has a complex history, beginning in 1937 as a small airfield, developing into a military base during the Second World War, and finally evolving into the sprawling airport that we see today. This rich tapestry of historical events has seemingly resulted in a series of hauntings that hint at a residual energy left behind from the past.

One of the most enduring tales from Toronto Pearson International Airport revolves around the apparition of a man dressed in an old-fashioned pilot's uniform. This spectral figure has been seen by numerous airport employees, usually in the late hours of the night when the airport is relatively quiet. Many report seeing him near the runways, looking out towards the planes taking off and landing, as if waiting for a flight that never arrives.

An account from a long-serving maintenance worker, Malcolm, gives a chilling account of his encounter with this apparition. Working late one night, he noticed a figure standing near the edge of the runway. "He was dressed in an old-style pilot's uniform," Malcolm recalls. "He stood there, staring out at the runway. It was quite foggy, and there was something about him that just didn't feel right. I called out to him, but he didn't respond. I turned around for a moment to grab my radio, and when I looked back, he was gone. Vanished into thin air."

In addition to the spectral pilot, there have been numerous reports of mysterious noises throughout the airport. These phantom sounds include disembodied voices, echoing footsteps, and the distant hum of an aeroplane engine when no planes are due to take off or land. The source of these sounds remains unexplained, adding another layer of mystery to the airport.

One such incident was reported by an air traffic controller named Clara. She recalls a night when she heard the distinct sound of a plane approaching the runway. However, when she checked her radar, no aircraft were in the vicinity. "It was as clear as day, the sound of a plane engine," she says. "I double-checked the radar, and there was nothing. It was as if an invisible plane was making its descent."

Beyond the apparition of the pilot and the unexplained sounds, there are stories of objects moving on their own and lights flickering inexplicably. One tale comes from a baggage handler, Luis, who had a chilling experience in the baggage claim area. "I was loading luggage onto the conveyor belt," he says, "and I placed a suitcase next to me. When I turned to grab it, it was at the other end of the belt. There was no one else around. It was as if the suitcase moved on its own."

These accounts, coupled with the airport's rich history, have fostered an atmosphere of mystery and intrigue within the walls of Toronto Pearson International Airport. The sightings of the spectral pilot, the unexplained sounds, the objects moving on their own, and the flickering lights are all part of the airport's tapestry of ghostly tales.

These stories, like the whispers of a forgotten past, are interwoven with the daily operations of this bustling airport. As travellers hurry to catch their flights, baggage handlers load suitcases, and air traffic controllers monitor the skies, these eerie
phenomena linger, casting an ethereal veil over the everyday routine.

The apparition of the old-time pilot, ever-watchful, stands as a poignant symbol of the airport's historical lineage, a spectral reminder of the people who've been part of its journey through the years. The disembodied sounds, the humming of phantom planes, the echoing footsteps, seem to reverberate with the echoes of a vibrant past, a sonic imprint of the airport's multifaceted history.

Similarly, the inexplicable movement of objects and flickering lights contribute to the uncanny aura that envelops the airport. These seemingly random incidents hint at the possibility of unseen forces at play, suggesting that the airport could be a hotspot of residual energy, an epicentre where the past and present converge in inexplicable ways.

Despite the eerie nature of these occurrences, the airport staff have come to accept these oddities as part of their work environment. Many view these incidents with a sense of awe and respect, recognizing them as manifestations of the airport's storied past. For these individuals, the spectral pilot, the phantom sounds, and the mysteriously moving objects serve as reminders that they are mere custodians of a place with a rich historical legacy and a vibrant, if somewhat eerie, life of its own.

As the tales of Toronto Pearson International Airport unfold, they invite us to explore the intricate web of stories that underpin these modern hubs of transit. They challenge us to broaden our understanding of these spaces, urging us to look beyond the physical structures and acknowledge the unseen layers that contribute to their unique character.

In the grand scheme of things, airports are more than just gateways for travel. They are living, breathing entities, repositories of countless personal stories, historical events, and, as it seems, a fair share of spectral occurrences. As such, they serve as poignant reminders of our collective journey through time, mirroring our evolution, our triumphs, and our losses.

As we delve deeper into the realm of the unexplained, we find that these stories offer a unique perspective on our understanding of reality. They raise intriguing questions about the nature of existence, the persistence of memory, and the possibility of a life beyond the physical world.

The unexplained happenings at Toronto Pearson International Airport are but a chapter in the broader narrative of haunted airports around the world. Yet, they encapsulate the very essence of this journey into the unknown, challenging us to question, to seek, and, most importantly, to marvel at the mysteries that surround us.

The Shadowy Figures of Rome's Fiumicino Airport

The Eternal City of Rome is a repository of the ancient and the modern, where centuries-old ruins stand tall amidst bustling streets and contemporary architecture. It's an urban landscape steeped in history and teeming with life, a place where the echoes of a glorious past reverberate in the present. Yet, Rome's historical legacy extends beyond its city boundaries, seeping into spaces that might seem unlikely repositories of spectral pasts. One such place is the city's largest airport, the Fiumicino Airport, also known as Leonardo da Vinci Airport.

Officially opened on January 15, 1961, Fiumicino Airport has grown to become one of the busiest airports in Europe. Over the decades, it has witnessed countless goodbyes and reunions, farewells and welcomes, joyous beginnings and poignant endings. It's a vibrant space, pulsating with the energy of human emotion and endeavour. Yet, like many other airports, Fiumicino has a shadowy underside that belies its bustling exterior. Over the years, there have been numerous accounts of unexplained phenomena, particularly involving spectral figures that seem to flit in and out of existence, casting an eerie pall over the airport's vibrant landscape.

One such haunting encounter involves an entity known as "The Man in the Brown Overcoat." Over the years, several passengers and airport staff have reported spotting a tall man, dressed in an outdated brown overcoat and hat, wandering the terminals. The man is often seen standing in corners, silently observing the bustling activity around him. When approached, he vanishes, leaving behind a chilling gust of wind that sends shivers down the spine.

Another spectral figure that has been sighted multiple times is a woman dressed in a 1960s flight attendant uniform. She is often seen in the early hours of the morning, walking down deserted corridors with a melancholic expression. Numerous staff members have reported hearing a soft, sorrowful humming emanating from her direction, a haunting melody that resonates in the silence of the pre-dawn hours.

Then there are accounts of ghostly figures seen on the runways, sometimes appearing in front of incoming flights, causing startled pilots to swerve at the last moment. These spectral apparitions often resemble pilots or ground staff from bygone eras, their uniforms outdated and their expressions marked by an enduring sadness.

The shadowy figures of Fiumicino are not just confined to human forms. There have been numerous reports of phantom planes that appear on the radar, only to vanish within seconds. Air traffic controllers have reported hearing cryptic messages over the radio, often in languages that haven't been used in aviation for decades. These unexplained incidents have added another layer to Fiumicino's reputation as a space where the past and present intertwine in inexplicable ways.

It's not just the apparitions that lend an eerie aura to Fiumicino. Passengers and staff have often reported a sudden drop in temperature in certain parts of the airport, particularly around the old Terminal 2. There have also been instances of unexplained noises echoing through the terminals late at night – the sound of footsteps, the rustling of papers, even the distant laughter of children.

In attempting to understand these spectral occurrences, one

cannot ignore the airport's historical context. Rome is a city steeped in history and Fiumicino, despite being a relatively recent addition to the city's landscape, is no exception. The land on which the airport is built has been the site of numerous archaeological discoveries, including an ancient Roman necropolis that was unearthed during the airport's expansion in the 1990s.

While it's tempting to attribute these hauntings to the presence of this ancient burial ground, the spectral figures sighted at Fiumicino do not conform to the attire or appearance of ancient Roman spirits. Instead, they seem to hail from more recent times, suggesting that the airport's own history might be the source of these hauntings.

Fiumicino, in its six decades of operation, has been the site of numerous incidents, some tragic, others fraught with emotional upheaval. It's a place where emotions run high, where the joy of reunions mingles with the sorrow of partings, where hopes are kindled and dreams are shattered. It's these intense emotional imprints, some believe, that might have given rise to the airport's spectral inhabitants. These shadowy figures might be remnants of the airport's past, trapped in a temporal loop, forever reenacting their final moments.

The Man in the Brown Overcoat, for instance, has often been sighted near the arrivals area. Could he be a spirit waiting for a loved one who never arrived? The woman in the flight attendant uniform, with her melancholic demeanour and sorrowful humming, might she be mourning a life cut short in its prime? And the ghostly figures on the runways, could they be remnants of a tragic incident, forever replaying their final moments?

As for the phantom planes and cryptic radio messages, they add another layer to the airport's spectral tapestry. They seem to echo a time when aviation was in its infancy, a time fraught with risks and uncertainties, where every flight was a journey into the unknown. Could these phantom planes be echoes of flights that never reached their destination, trapped in a perpetual cycle of takeoffs and landings?

The shadowy figures of Fiumicino Airport offer a tantalising glimpse into the airport's spectral underworld. They're a reminder that every place has a story to tell, a history that extends beyond the visible and tangible. They're testament to the idea that the past lingers on, its echoes reverberating in the present, sometimes taking on forms that defy our understanding of time and space.

As you traverse the bustling terminals of Fiumicino Airport, amidst the clamour of announcements and the hum of activity, spare a thought for its spectral inhabitants. Look beyond the apparent and you might catch a glimpse of the Man in the Brown Overcoat standing in a corner, or hear the sorrowful humming of the ghostly flight attendant. You might feel a sudden chill as you walk past Terminal 2, or hear the faint echo of children's laughter in the silence of the night.

The shadowy figures of Fiumicino Airport serve as a poignant reminder of the airport's spectral past, a past that continues to coexist with the present in ways that challenge our perception of reality. They're a testament to the idea that airports, despite their modern façade, are spaces where history, emotion, and mystery intertwine, creating a tapestry that's as fascinating as it is eerie.

So, the next time you find yourself at Fiumicino, pause for a moment. Look around. Listen. You might just find yourself experiencing the airport's spectral side, a side that adds a whole new dimension to the airport's identity. It might just change the way you perceive airports, transforming them from mere transit points to portals into the realm of the unknown, where the past lingers on and the spectral coexists with the corporeal.

The Eerie Whispers of Hong Kong International Airport

Hong Kong International Airport, a marvel of modern architectural prowess, stands as a beacon of human advancement in the heart of Asia. Despite its resplendent facades and ceaseless hum of activity, there's an ethereal layer to this transportation hub that defies its modernity. From the whispering winds navigating the colossal terminals to the spectral echoes reverberating through its long, desolate corridors, this airport houses an array of ghostly manifestations that have provoked a mixture of fear, intrigue, and fascination.

The airport, locally known as Chek Lap Kok Airport, owes its name to the island it was built upon. Before the airport's existence, the island was a serene fishing village. The villagers, displaced by the construction, had to abandon their ancestral homes, leaving behind memories that, to this day, seem to echo in the form of ghostly whispers throughout the airport.

These spectral whispers have become an integral part of the airport's folklore, with countless passengers and staff reporting experiences of being called out by name, hearing fragmented conversations, and even being warned of potential dangers. One such account comes from a long-serving member of the airport staff, Liu. He recounts being alone in the baggage handling area late at night when he heard a whisper in his ear warning him to "step back." He instinctively followed the instruction, narrowly missing a malfunctioning piece of machinery. There was no one around who could have issued the warning.

The whispers, however, are not the only eerie occurrences. Multiple sightings of apparitions have been reported, painting a spectral canvas that is as diverse as it is chilling. One such recurring entity is a woman dressed in traditional Chinese clothing. Often sighted during the wee hours near the departure gates, her ethereal figure exudes an overwhelming sense of melancholy. Some believe her to be a former resident of the island, eternally wandering the land she once called home.

Another spectral entity that roams the airport is an elderly man, often seen near the check-in counters. He appears to be searching for something, rummaging through trash bins and looking around in seeming desperation. He's been approached by staff members on multiple occasions, only to vanish before their eyes. One theory suggests he could be a restless spirit in search of a lost belonging or perhaps waiting for a loved one who never arrived.

There's also the tale of a spectral pilot who haunts the runways. Described as a figure clad in an old-fashioned pilot's uniform, he's often seen looking out toward the planes taking off and landing, his figure illuminated by the glow of the runway lights. The spectral pilot never interacts with the living, seemingly stuck in his own time and place, perhaps waiting for a flight that will never come.

In addition to these frequent hauntings, there are countless one-off stories that add to the airport's spectral lore. From ghostly faces appearing in restroom mirrors to unexplained cold spots and feelings of being watched, the airport has seen it all.

One particularly bone-chilling account comes from a frequent traveller, Mei, who claims to have seen a spectral child in one of the airport's play areas late at night. The ghostly child was playing alone, laughing in the unnerving silence of the deserted terminal. As Mei approached, the child looked up, gave her a sad smile, and vanished, leaving behind an empty playground and a chilling memory that Mei claims she'll carry to her grave.

Through these spectral whispers, apparitions, and eerie encounters, the Hong Kong International Airport presents a fascinating interplay of the modern and the mystical, the physical and the spectral. It stands as a testament to the idea that places, like people, are shaped by their past and carry echoes of their history into the present, manifesting in ways that defy our understanding of reality. The airport is not just a hub for physical journeys across the globe but also a crossroads for spiritual encounters that blur the lines between this world and the next.

As these stories continue to echo through the bustling terminals, they serve as reminders of the airport's historical and emotional depth, reaching beyond the tangible and into the realm of the unknown. Every whisper, every apparition, every spectral encounter, adds another layer to the airport's mystical tapestry, weaving a narrative of spectral existence that parallels the daily humdrum of human activity.

One haunting account comes from a late-night janitor, Wong,

who recalls an encounter that forever changed his perspective on life and death. While cleaning one of the less-frequented restrooms, he heard soft whispers coming from one of the stalls. Assuming it was a stranded traveller, he knocked on the door, offering assistance. The whispers stopped, and the door creaked open to reveal an empty stall. Wong swears that he saw a fleeting shadow disappear under the restroom's fluorescent lighting.

Spectral encounters aren't limited to just staff and nocturnal wanderers. Several travellers have also reported uncanny experiences. A British tourist named Evelyn recalls waiting for her delayed flight when she heard a soft whisper in her ear saying, "Go home." Startled, she turned around to find no one near her. The whisper repeated thrice before it stopped. Evelyn later learned that her father had passed away around the same time back home, leading her to believe that it was his spirit urging her to return.

Tales of ghostly whispers and eerie encounters at the Hong Kong International Airport continue to intrigue and unsettle those who pass through its corridors. Some choose to dismiss these accounts as products of fatigue, stress, or tricks of light and sound. But those who've experienced these spectral phenomena hold firm in their belief, asserting the existence of an uncanny realm that coexists with our own.

As the narratives of ghostly whispers and apparitions continue to circulate, they become part of the airport's rich tapestry of tales, blurring the lines between hearsay and reality, between dismissible fiction and undeniable experiences. The airport, in all its modern grandeur, serves as a spectral theatre, playing out ghostly dramas that hint at the untold stories of its past and the invisible threads that tie the present to the yonder.

In the end, the Hong Kong International Airport, with its spectral whispers and eerie encounters, serves as a potent reminder of the unseen dimensions of our existence. Amid the hustle and bustle of human life, in the liminal spaces of departures and arrivals, life and death, the seen and unseen, it invites us to listen closely, to perceive more deeply, to open ourselves to the possibility of a reality that extends beyond what meets the eye.

Whether it's the chilling whispers echoing through the terminals, the spectral figures wandering aimlessly, or the inexplicable cold spots and vanishing figures, these accounts imbue the airport with a spectral character that surpasses its physical existence. Hong Kong International Airport emerges as a haunted hotspot where the living and the dead continue to intersect, telling a chilling tale of coexistence that remains as haunting as the spectral whispers that echo through its sprawling expanse.

The Haunted Control Tower of San Francisco International Airport

San Francisco International Airport, the seventh busiest airport in the United States, is a sprawling complex of terminals, runways, and hangars, bustling with ceaseless activity. However, nestled within this hub of human activity, the airport's control tower stands as a spectral beacon of eerie phenomena, its history intertwined with chilling tales of unexplained sounds and the persistent sightings of a mysterious figure.

The control tower, with its panoramic views of the runways, taxiways, and apron areas, is the nerve centre of the airport. Air traffic controllers work around the clock to ensure the safe and efficient movement of aircraft. The work is demanding and requires an acute focus on the task at hand. But for decades, controllers at San Francisco International Airport have been periodically distracted from their duties by strange occurrences that defy rational explanation.

The most prevalent of these phenomena are the inexplicable sounds that echo through the tower during the graveyard shift. Controllers have reported hearing footsteps in the stairwell when no one is there, doors opening and closing on their own, and a persistent tapping sound that seems to originate from within the walls. These eerie sounds, often heard in the dead of night when the airport is at its quietest, have unsettled even the most hardened controllers.

Perhaps the most chilling tale is that of the mysterious figure that has been sighted on numerous occasions in the control tower. This apparition, often seen out of the corner of the eye, appears as a shadowy figure moving swiftly through the tower before vanishing into thin air. Controllers who have encountered this figure describe a sense of profound unease, a feeling that they are not alone.

One controller, Thomas, vividly recalls his encounter with the spectral figure. He was working the late shift when he saw a dark figure darting past him in his peripheral vision. Turning around, he found no one there. This happened several times throughout his shift, each time sending a chill down his spine. He later found out that many of his colleagues had similar experiences, and the figure had become something of a legend among the controllers.

Another compelling account comes from Maria, a veteran air traffic controller, who encountered the mysterious figure one night while working alone in the tower. She saw a shadowy figure standing by the window, overlooking the runways. When she called out, the figure disappeared. Shaken but determined to rationalise what she had seen, Maria continued with her duties. However, the figure reappeared multiple times throughout her shift, each time vanishing as she tried to get a closer look.

The stories of unexplained sounds and sightings have been a part of the control tower's lore for years, passed down from one generation of controllers to the next. These tales have become woven into the fabric of the tower's history, serving as chilling reminders of the tower's spectral reputation.

San Francisco International Airport has a rich history dating back to 1927, and the control tower has been a vital part of this history. Its strategic location and panoramic views have made it an ideal setting for strange occurrences. Whether these events are echoes of the past or manifestations of something beyond our understanding remains a mystery. What is undeniable, however, is the effect they have had on those who work within the tower's confines.

The haunted control tower of San Francisco International Airport serves as a potent reminder that even in the most technologically advanced and rational environments, there are phenomena that challenge our understanding of the world. The spectral figure and eerie sounds that echo through the tower continue to perplex and fascinate those who encounter them, adding a layer of mystery to the airport's history.

As the stories of the haunted control tower continue to be told, they add to the spectral character of San Francisco International Airport, intertwining the everyday operations with a tapestry of lingering mysteries and ghostly tales. The spectral figure and otherworldly sounds are not simply terrifying phenomena, they represent the unknown that lives side by side with the living, an enduring testament to the enigmatic side of human experience.

The tales of the haunted control tower have gained a certain legendary status among the staff at the airport. It's not uncommon for new air traffic controllers to be greeted with these stories on their first night shift, a kind of rite of passage into the enigmatic world that they now find themselves a part of. These narratives, told and retold over years, are now deeply ingrained in the culture of the airport, shaping the way the staff perceive their workspace, and adding an eerie, haunting texture to the environment.

Air traffic controller Lucas shared his own encounter which happened during one of his first graveyard shifts. Around 3 AM, he was jolted from his work by the sound of a door slowly creaking open. He turned around to see who was there, but he found nothing but an empty hallway. As he turned back to the control panel, he noticed a shadowy figure standing at the edge of his vision. He described it as a human silhouette, but when he attempted to focus on it, the figure vanished.

The experiences of these air traffic controllers serve as a stark reminder of the airport's spectral presence. The shadowy figure, the unexplained sounds, the feeling of being watched - all these incidents continue to add to the eeriness surrounding the airport's control tower.

Mia, a cleaner who's been working in the control tower for over a decade, has her own tales to tell. She's often heard a strange tapping sound coming from inside the walls of the tower. The first time she heard it, she assumed it was just the building settling, but over time, the rhythmic tapping became more pronounced, and always in the same spot. On one occasion, she saw a dark figure out of the corner of her eye, but when she turned to look, nothing was there. Since then, she's felt a certain chill every time she enters the tower, a distinct feeling of unease that she can't shake off.

The haunted control tower at San Francisco International Airport continues to be a source of fascination, not only for those who work there but also for those who hear its ghostly tales. Whether these phenomena are the echoes of past tragedies, manifestations of lingering spirits, or something else entirely, remains unknown. However, their existence is a stark reminder of the unseen world that coexists with ours, often unnoticed but occasionally making itself known in the most mysterious of ways.

The Restless Spirits of Mexico City International Airport

Mexico City International Airport, officially known as Benito Juarez International Airport, is one of the busiest airports in Latin America, seeing millions of passengers every year. However, this bustling transportation hub also harbours its share of eerie tales and unexplained phenomena that have been passed down through generations. This chapter focuses on the restless spirits that are said to inhabit the terminals of this airport, their spectral presence a stark contrast to the modern hustle and bustle of the environment.

The airport's history dates back to the early 20th century, a period marked by significant political and social changes in Mexico. As the city's main gateway to the world, the airport became a key location for countless human stories, from joyous reunions and tearful farewells to tragic accidents and unfulfilled dreams. It's perhaps no wonder, then, that such an emotionally charged place is believed to be inhabited by spirits unable to find peace.

One of the most well-known ghostly occurrences at Mexico City International Airport is the sighting of a spectral woman in Terminal 2. This apparition, often seen late at night or in the early hours of the morning, appears to be in distress. Dressed in a traditional Mexican outfit, she wanders the terminal, her transparent figure illuminated by the soft glow of the airport lights. Passengers and staff who've seen her report feeling a wave of sadness and despair emanating from the spirit, as if she's eternally searching for something or someone she's lost.

A janitor, who has worked at the airport for more than twenty years, shared his encounter with the spectral woman. He was working the night shift, cleaning the nearly empty terminal when he heard a woman's sobs echoing through the hallways. Following the sound, he came across the spectral figure. Overwhelmed by the profound sadness that the apparition radiated, he could do nothing but watch as she disappeared into the walls of the terminal.

In addition to the spectral woman, there have been multiple accounts of a ghostly child roaming the airport. The spirit is often seen playing near the departure gates and is described as a young boy, around seven or eight years old, dressed in period clothing. Unlike the spectral woman, the ghostly child appears to be carefree and oblivious to his surroundings.

One late-night traveller, while waiting for a delayed flight, reported seeing the spectral child playing with an old, worn-out ball near the departure gate. She watched as the boy kicked the ball, his laughter echoing through the terminal. When she tried to approach him, the child simply vanished, leaving behind nothing but an eerie silence.

The airport's control tower is another site of numerous ghostly encounters. Air traffic controllers, working late into the night, have reported hearing unexplained noises, including footsteps, whispers, and the sound of someone or something tapping on the window. On several occasions, controllers have seen a shadowy figure moving around in the tower, only for it to vanish when they tried to investigate.

One controller shared his chilling experience during a late-night shift. While monitoring the air traffic, he felt a sudden chill, and his radio began to emit static. Out of the corner of his eye, he saw a shadowy figure standing behind him. He quickly turned around, but there was no one there. However, the feeling of being watched persisted for the rest of his shift, leaving him in a state of unease.

The numerous ghostly sightings and unexplained phenomena at Mexico City International Airport add an eerie layer to the airport's rich history. The tales of the spectral woman, the ghostly child, and the shadowy figure in the control tower serve as reminders of the airport's spectral inhabitants, who, for reasons unknown, seem to be stuck in a liminal space, forever tethered to this transportation hub.

The spectral woman's profound sadness, the ghostly child's joyous play, and the shadowy figure's watchful presence in the control tower are all manifestations of the profound emotions and experiences that have unfolded within the airport's walls over the years. Each spirit seems to represent a different aspect of the human experience, from profound grief and loss to innocent joy and the lingering presence of those who were once integral to the airport's operations.

The tales of these restless spirits are passed down from one generation of airport staff to the next, becoming part of the airport's collective memory and lore. These stories, despite their eerie nature, add a layer of depth to the everyday occurrences at the airport, intertwining the ordinary with the extraordinary, the visible with the invisible, and the past with the present.

A former customs officer, retired after decades of service, once remarked that working at the airport was like "walking through a living history." The spectral woman, the ghostly child, and the shadowy figure in the control tower were, to him, echoes of the airport's past, manifestations of the countless human stories that had played out within its walls. Despite their ghostly nature, he saw them not as objects of fear, but as reminders of the airport's rich tapestry of human experiences.

The Mexico City International Airport's restless spirits continue to capture the imaginations of passengers and staff alike. Their spectral presence adds an eerie undercurrent to the airport's usual hustle and bustle, suggesting that there might be more to this modern transportation hub than meets the eye.

The airport, like many other places that have witnessed countless human stories, seems to retain an imprint of these past experiences, manifesting in the form of spectral sightings and unexplained phenomena. The haunted terminals and control tower stand as portals to the past, reminding us of the airport's enduring history and its spectral inhabitants who are unable to find peace.

The Ghostly Encounters at Singapore Changi Airport

Bustling with activity and home to stunning architecture, shopping complexes, and even a butterfly garden, Singapore Changi Airport is renowned for its excellence in providing a seamless and enjoyable travel experience. However, beyond the modern amenities and efficient services, lies a different narrative that is whispered among the airport staff and has been passed down from one generation to the next - a narrative that tells of spectral sightings, ghostly apparitions, and unexplained phenomena.

The origins of these eerie tales can be traced back to the airport's location. The land on which the airport stands was once a swampland with many lush plantations, and more ominously, it was a site where Japanese forces executed numerous prisoners during World War II. This tumultuous past has led some to believe that the airport might be haunted by the spirits of those who met their tragic end there.

One of the most enduring tales from Changi Airport is the sighting of a ghostly old woman. Over the years, numerous airport staff and even some passengers have reported seeing an elderly woman wandering in and around the airport, particularly late at night when the flow of human traffic is low. Cloaked in traditional attire, she is often seen praying or whispering to herself in the older terminals. Despite numerous attempts by security personnel to approach her, she seemingly vanishes into thin air, leaving no trace behind.

The tale of the ghostly old woman is not the only spectral story that pervades the airport. Another eerie tale that has been passed down among the airport staff is the sighting of a young boy. The boy, who appears to be around five years old, is often seen playing near the departure gates. He is always alone and seems to be engrossed in his play, oblivious to the hustle and bustle around him. Passengers who have tried to approach him have reported that he simply disappears, leaving them bewildered and questioning their own perceptions.

In addition to these spectral sightings, there are numerous

accounts of unexplained phenomena at Changi Airport. Luggage trolleys moving on their own, lights flickering without any apparent electrical issues, and even announcements being made over the public address system when no one is in the control room are some of the mysterious incidents that have been reported. These occurrences, while they could be attributed to technical glitches, have added to the airport's spectral lore due to their inexplicable nature.

The experiences of those who work the night shift at the airport are particularly chilling. From cleaners and security personnel to ground staff, many have reported feeling an inexplicable chill, hearing faint whispers, or even feeling a ghostly touch. These experiences, while unsettling, have become an integral part of working at Changi Airport, adding a spectral dimension to the everyday workings of this bustling transportation hub.

Despite the modernity and efficiency that Singapore Changi Airport is renowned for, the tales of ghostly apparitions and unexplained phenomena serve as a stark reminder of the airport's history and its connection with the past. Each sighting, each ecrie occurrence, and each unexplained incident adds to the narrative of the airport, infusing the everyday with elements of the extraordinary.

These tales, while unsettling, add a layer of complexity to the airport, intertwining the past with the present, the visible with the invisible, and the ordinary with the extraordinary. They serve as a testament to the idea that even in the most modern and bustling environments, the echoes of bygone eras continue to resonate, and the spectral inhabitants of these spaces continue to make their presence known in unexpected ways.

Through the stories of the ghostly old woman, the playful young boy, and the unexplained phenomena, we are invited to explore the spectral side of Singapore Changi Airport. These stories challenge our understanding of the world around us and invite us to delve into the unseen and the mysterious.

The spectral tales from Changi Airport are not merely ghost stories, they are narratives that explore the airport's past, its relationship with death and memory, and the ways in which these elements permeate the present. They challenge us to confront the unseen and the unknown, and to question the boundaries of our own perceptions.

The story of the elderly woman is a poignant reminder of the airport's past. Her ethereal presence, seen but not heard, speaks volumes about the history of the land on which the airport now stands. Her silent prayers, heard only by those who are willing to listen, echo the prayers of those who met their tragic end at this location during the war. She serves as a spectral reminder of the past, a past that refuses to be forgotten.

Similarly, the tale of the young boy is a chilling testament to the idea that the past continues to live on in the present, in ways that are both unsettling and mysterious. His innocent play in the midst of the bustling airport serves as a stark contrast to the tragic history of the airport's location, blurring the boundaries between past and present, life and death.

The unexplained phenomena that occur at the airport are, in many ways, reminders of the airport's spectral inhabitants. The moving luggage trolleys, the flickering lights, and the ghostly announcements are manifestations of the unseen, the unheard, and the unknown. They serve as reminders that in the midst of the mundane and the everyday, the spectral and the extraordinary continue to make their presence known.

Through the tales of ghostly apparitions and unexplained phenomena at Singapore Changi Airport, we gain a deeper understanding of the airport's history, its relationship with the past, and the ways in which this past continues to permeate the present. The spectral tales challenge our understanding of the world around us and invite us to delve into the unseen and the unknown, to question the boundaries of our own perceptions, and to explore the complex interplay between past and present, visible and invisible, ordinary and extraordinary.

The spectral tales from Changi Airport are not just ghost stories, but narratives that explore the airport's past, its relationship with death and memory, and the ways in which these elements permeate the present. They challenge us to confront the unseen and the unknown, and to question the boundaries of our own perceptions.

In the end, the ghostly tales from Singapore Changi Airport remind us that no place, no matter how modern or bustling, is immune from the echoes of its past. They serve as a testament to the power of memory and the enduring presence of the spectral, reminding us that in the most unexpected places, the past continues to resonate, and the dead continue to make their presence known.

Afterword

As we conclude our journey through the spectral terminals and haunted runways of the world's most mysterious airports, it's worth pausing to reflect on the remarkable stories we've traversed. Within these chapters, we've navigated the interstices between the seen and unseen, the known and unknown, the living and the dead. We've delved into eerie encounters and unnerving phenomena that challenge our perceptions and invite us to question the boundaries of our reality.

Each airport we visited unveiled its unique ghostly narratives, bound to its past and resonating in its present. From the phantom pilots of Denver International Airport to the ghostly encounters at Singapore Changi Airport, we've borne witness to tales that speak of a spectral reality co-existing with our own.

The phantom flight attendants of Dallas/Fort Worth International Airport, the restless spirits of Tenerife North Airport, and the tragic spirits of Mexico City International

Airport, among others, represent an enduring memory of a past that refuses to be forgotten, forever imprinted on the fabric of these bustling transportation hubs. Their spectral presence, their unseen existence, and their haunting narratives serve as stark reminders of the profound interplay between life, death, and memory.

In the crying child of Heathrow Airport and the lost souls of Charles de Gaulle Airport, we encounter narratives of longing and loss. Their spectral presence echoes the profound human emotions of grief and sorrow, of longing and yearning, reminding us of the inseparable link between the emotional and the spectral. These stories challenge us to consider the depth of human emotions and their capacity to resonate beyond the realm of the living.

We traversed the spectral landscape of Madrid-Barajas Airport, haunted by the enigmatic Lady in White, and the haunted halls of Berlin-Tegel Airport, resonating with its Cold War history. These tales underscore the intricate ways in which personal narratives and historical events intertwine, giving rise to spectral tales that defy time and space.

The eerie whispers of Hong Kong International Airport, the

shadowy figures of Rome's Fiumicino Airport, and the ghostly soldiers of Okinawa's Naha Airport offered a glimpse into a world that lingers at the edges of our perception. These hauntings, experienced by both staff and passengers alike, challenge our understanding of reality, inviting us to consider the existence of a realm that exists beyond our ordinary perception.

In the haunting tales from Toronto Pearson International Airport and the spectral narratives from San Francisco International Airport's control tower, we've encountered stories that defy logical explanation. The unexplained happenings and mysterious apparitions invite us to question the nature of reality and the limitations of our understanding.

Throughout our exploration of these haunted airports, we've learned that these are not just places of transit, but spaces imbued with meaning, history, and memory. Each spectral tale, each ghostly encounter, each unexplained phenomenon, is a testament to the enduring presence of the past in the present, the visible in the invisible, and the known in the unknown.

As we conclude our journey, it's important to remember that these spectral tales are not simply ghost stories, but narratives that explore the profound interplay between life and death, memory and oblivion, the mundane and the extraordinary. They challenge us to confront our fears, question our perceptions, and explore the boundaries of our understanding.

In the end, "Haunted Airports" is more than just a collection of ghost stories. It's a journey into the unseen and the unknown, an exploration of the spectral dimensions of our reality, and an invitation to engage with the world around us in ways that transcend the ordinary.

As you close this book, remember the spectral tales you've encountered and the haunting narratives you've traversed. Let them invite you to look beyond the surface, to seek the unseen, to delve into the unknown, and to challenge the boundaries of your understanding. Keep these stories close, let them transform your perspective, and remember that every airport, every terminal, every runway, carries with it a spectral tale waiting to be discovered. As you embark on your next journey, look closely, listen carefully, and you might just encounter the spectral presence that lingers in the shadows, forever echoing the tales within these pages.

"Haunted Airports" thus offers you not just a collection of

chilling tales, but a new lens to view the world, a reminder of the echoes of the past, and an invitation to embrace the mysteries of the unknown. As you conclude this journey, may it inspire you to explore, question, and seek the unseen, carrying with you the awareness of the spectral world that coexists with our own. With this, we conclude our spectral journey, leaving you with an enriched perspective and an awakened curiosity to explore the spectral narratives that lie in wait, wherever your journeys may take you.

Thank you for buying this book!

Lee Brickley has written and published more than 20 books on the paranormal which are all available from Amazon right now. Just search "Lee Brickley" to discover more about the weird and often terrifying world of the supernatural :)

Printed in Great Britain
by Amazon